Praise for *Leadership Rules*

"Once again Chris Widener provides the reader a fascinating story. The reader will savor time-tested principles of leadership by example. This is a must-read in the arsenal of any aspiring leader!"
—**David Humphrey**, president, ILD Global

"I love books that have business stories with meaningful takeaways. They're fun to read yet provide actions that help improve me and my business. Chris Widener's *Leadership Rules* is a simple read with simple, practical rules that will help you become a better leader of people."
—**Tony Alessandra**, author, *The NEW Art of Managing People* and *The Platinum Rule*

"Fundamental principles captured in a warm-hearted story line. Quickly digested. Harder to apply. Recommended for those who intend to create cultures of personal responsibility and winners in business and life."
—**Dianna Booher**, author, *The Voices of Authority* and *Booher's Rules of Business Grammar*

LEADERSHIP RULES

HOW TO BECOME THE LEADER YOU WANT TO BE

Chris Widener

JOSSEY-BASS
A Wiley Imprint
www.josseybass.com

Published by Jossey-Bass
A Wiley Imprint
989 Market Street, San Francisco, CA 94103-1741   www.josseybass.com

Jossey-Bass books and products are available through most bookstores. To contact Jossey-Bass directly call our Customer Care Department within the U.S. at 800-956-7739, outside the U.S. at 317-572-3986, or fax 317-572-4002.

Jossey-Bass also publishes its books in a variety of electronic formats. Some content that appears in print may not be available in electronic books.

Library of Congress Cataloging-in-Publication Data

Widener, Chris.
  Leadership rules : how to become the leader you want to be / Chris Widener.
    p.   cm.
  ISBN 978-0-470-91472-4 (hardback); ISBN 978-0-470-93167-7 (ebk);
  ISBN 978-0-470-93169-1 (ebk); ISBN 978-0-470-93170-7 (ebk)
    1. Leadership.   I. Title.
  HD57.7.W523   2010
  658.4'092—dc22

                                                          2010036006

Printed in the United States of America
FIRST EDITION
HB Printing   10 9 8 7 6 5 4 3 2 1

CONTENTS

Introduction 1

THE STORY 4

THE LESSONS 128

Acknowledgments 167
About the Author 169

INTRODUCTION

Every time I start writing a new book, I am reminded of Solomon's words: *Of the writing of books, there is no end*. I ask myself if there is really a purpose for writing the book that I am about to write. If there isn't, I don't.

Ultimately, I write a book because I want to help people learn something or be reminded of something. I love the old line from G. K. Chesterton that says that people need to be reminded more than they need to be instructed. This is where I spend most of my time: Reminding people. Most of the time I am not saying something new; rather I am reminding my readers of something they have probably heard already. My goal is to remind them, often in a fresh way through a unique story, of the truths that govern successful living.

Simplicity is the key to success. Success isn't brain surgery. As I write a book about leadership, I am even more convinced than ever that leadership is simple. It is hard, but it is simple.

Leadership Rules is about the simplicity of leadership. If you want to lead people, if you want to influence people and move them toward a common goal—whether it is a family, a business, or a football team—a few simple rules will form the foundation for that leadership.

One last thought. I use the word *rules* very specifically. It is human nature to want the easy answer, the silver bullet. We don't want the rule, we want the law. The problem is that with human behavior, which leadership is completely beholden to, there is no one way. There are no laws that govern human behavior. Neither I nor anyone else can tell you that if you do thus and so, it will work all the time. That just isn't so. Human behavior is extraordinarily complex.

And there's the rub. It is complex, *and* it is simple. If you have a group of a thousand people that you lead, you have tens of thousands of variables that are taking place in their lives that shape them and the way they will respond to your leadership. It is entirely impossible to fully meet the problem of complexity as you attempt to lead. Yet the good news is that there are a few simple rules that, if followed, will meet the needs of most of the people, most of the time.

In the following pages, I hope to remind you of some simple truths that will take you a long way in working with people and becoming a great leader. They will not work all of the time: people will fail, and even those closest to you will disappoint you from time to time. But if you implement these leadership rules you will become a better leader. You will gain a deeper influence in the lives of more people. And that will take you—and them—much further down the road of success.

PART ONE

THE STORY

CHAPTER 1

It is such a unique sound, the crunch of gravel under tires. That's the sound Mike Keller heard, and he didn't like it much.

It wouldn't have been so bad except that it was his driveway. His new driveway. The driveway to the house he wished he wasn't moving into. Born and raised in Chicago, he had no desire to live in Texas—but here he was, the newest resident of East Creek, Texas, about an hour outside of Dallas. To him, it might as well have been an hour out of Podunk.

What in the world am I doing here? he thought as he and his son Billy drove down the short driveway to the three-bedroom rambler he'd rented sight unseen. The one thing he did like about the house was that it was cheap, cheap, cheap. Especially compared to what housing cost in Chicago.

As the car rolled to a stop, Mike and Billy took in the scene. The paint was chipping, and one of the window screens was falling out. The screen door on the front entrance was swinging back and forth in the wind. The front yard didn't have a shred of green left in the grass. *Yep, this is Texas in August, all right.*

"Well son, here we are."

"Yep. . . . Here we are."

Billy's resignation was obvious. The kid had been no more pleased than you could expect about being pulled away from his friends in high school, but he'd been a good sport about it, sticking by his choice to live with his father when his parents split up. Mike and Billy had been baching it for the last year or so, ever since Mike's wife, Kristy, had announced that she wanted a separation.

Maybe the distance will do us all some good, Mike thought. He and Kristy had been trying for a reconciliation but talking different languages, and Mike's job at Markston Machine Corporation had been going poorly on top of it. The stress had been so bad, anything might be an improvement. Mike opened the car door and stood up, feeling like he'd stepped into an oven. "Let's leave the stuff in the car for now, son, and get the lay of the land in the house first." The movers would be there the next day, but Mike and Billy had brought down a carload of things to make the place barely habitable.

"Okay," Billy replied.

They hurried up the cracked walkway. Mike stuck the key in and opened the door. "Our new domain," he said.

It was musty inside. Very hot. Cobwebs in the corners. They tried the window air conditioner, but it just sputtered, making about twice as much noise as cold air.

"I'll open some windows," Billy said. "It's worse in here than outside."

"Good idea." *I'll have to buy an air conditioner*, Mike thought. *Or three.*

The two of them just stood there in the middle of the empty living room, dripping sweat. "I know this is tough, son," Mike said as he pulled Billy into a hug. "We'll make it, though. Everything happens for a reason, and we just have to figure out what the lesson is here."

"I know."

"You know, there is an old quote I like. When the student is ready, the teacher will appear. Let's be ready for what we are supposed to learn here."

"What do you suppose it is, Dad?"

"I have no idea, son, no idea whatsoever." Mike was feeling as lost as he ever had. Wondering how to save his marriage, how to recoup his failing career, how to be what he had always hoped he would be.

It had been a month since Tom Markston, the third-generation CEO of Markston Machine, had called Mike into his office. The conversation was a blur. Mike figured out quickly it wasn't good and only caught bits and pieces of it:

Things aren't working out here . . .

We thought you would be better prepared . . .

The fast-track option to leadership isn't going to happen here . . .

We think you need to relearn a few things . . .

You will be reassigned to the plant in . . . East Creek, Texas. . . .

Next thing they knew, Mike and Billy were in Texas. Mike had been demoted to the East Creek plant. It had been in the company for forty years, doing a lot of machine work that got distributed throughout the country. It was a small but integral part of the overall mission of MMC, but Mike knew being sent down to take over the plant was a demotion nonetheless.

The plant had about twelve hundred workers, making it a big fish in a town of fifteen thousand. But as a VP in Chicago, Mike had had more than four thousand people under him. Tom Markston had told Mike that the top team thought he needed to learn to become a better leader, so they were sending him to learn from the twelve hundred folks in East Creek that would now call him "Boss."

Mike thought it would have been a better idea to send him to an executive leadership program at Wharton or someplace else, but Tom said what he needed was hands-on work. He'd been pushed ahead too quickly, and now he needed to go backward before he could go forward again.

And that's how he and Billy ended up that summer, roasting in East Creek, Texas.

CHAPTER 2

After getting their carload of stuff inside and going out for pizza (and air-conditioning), Mike and Billy settled in to spend their first night on the living room floor. With no TV to watch, they just talked awhile. Eventually they fell asleep, their big adventure about to begin.

The next day they had a few things on their agenda before the movers showed up, the primary one being getting Billy signed up for football. He had played since he was eight and was pretty good. He wasn't D-1 college football material, but they figured he could probably walk on at a smaller school and get on the team. He was a decent size. Five foot eleven and a hundred and eighty pounds. He wasn't going to crush anyone, but he wouldn't be blown over either. The move had come up so quickly that neither Billy nor Mike had done any research about the football program at East Creek; they just figured it had to have one. Mike had never been to the town before. He'd never even been to Texas except to transfer planes through DFW. So they just showed up at East Creek High School and went to the office to register. After plowing through the paperwork, Billy asked about the football team and how to join.

"Practice starts next week," the secretary said. "You better get out to talk to Coach Logan. He's in his office in the gym."

Mike and Billy walked to the gym and knocked on a door that said "Coach" on it. No name, just "Coach."

"It's open," came the reply. They walked in.

"Are you the football coach?" Mike asked.

"That's me." He stood up from behind his desk and moved toward them. He was a big guy. Mike figured six foot two, two thirty. Extending his hand to Mike, he said, "Coach Logan. Brock Logan." They shook hands and then Coach turned to Billy to shake hands. As they did, the city elitist in Mike came out so fast he was just glad he didn't say it out loud. *Oh boy, "Brock Logan." We really are in Texas, aren't we? I wonder if this guy rides a horse to work.*

14

Coach looked Billy up and down. "Looks like you could be a weak safety."

"I played middle linebacker up in Chicago."

"This here ain't Chicago, Billy. My middle linebacker is six one, two-oh-five. All State as a junior last year. Can you punt?"

"Punt?"

"Yeah, kick the ball. Punt. We're weak there this year."

Mike stepped in. "Billy isn't a punter. He's played—and started—for a few years and played linebacker. Really, though, he'll play where he fits in once he gets the pads on. He's just looking to play a little football."

Coach got a grim smile on his face. "Don't nobody here play a little football, sir. When did you move here?"

"Yesterday. We just got in."

"Do you know anything about the program here, either of you?"

"No, my transfer came a short time ago and it's been so quick . . ."

"Where you work, Mike?"

"MMC. I'm the new plant manager. Twelve hundred people here work there."

"Yep, I heard old man Jones was retiring. Didn't know they were bringing in a city boy to pretty the place up, though. You must be good."

"I'd like to think so. It is the biggest thing in town."

Coach chuckled. "Mike, now that's where you are wrong. MMC is the *second*-biggest thing in town."

Mike thought to himself. He was sure that MMC was the biggest employer in East Creek. *All right, I'll bite.* "So what's the biggest thing in town?"

"Can't do all your work for you, Mike. You need to ask around." Coach handed Billy a clipboard. "Put your address here, Billy. You'll get paperwork on the program in the mail. Just be ready to go Monday morning."

"What time?"

"That'll be in the paperwork. I'll say this, though. Probably earlier than you've ever been up." He turned back to his desk. "Good to meet you folks. Billy, I'll see you Monday. Come to win."

"You mean come to play, right?" Billy asked.

"Nope. We don't *play*. We *win*. Come to win." With that, Coach pulled his reading glasses down, picked up some papers and began to read. Mike and Billy turned and let themselves out.

As they walked to the car, Mike said, "Typical good ol' boy. I'm sure he'll grow on us, though. You'll do all right."

"Yeah, he seemed a bit rough."

"He has to play the role of tough guy. He's the cowboy. Remember, this is Texas. Rural Texas at that."

They got in the car. "I wonder what he meant by your plant being the second-biggest thing in town? I thought you said you were the biggest employer in town."

"I don't know, son. I'll ask around. Maybe they have the world's best cherry pie down at the diner or something."

"Now *that* sounds good!"

"It sure does. Hey, do you mind if we drive by the plant? I need to check on a few things. We still have an hour before the movers are supposed to get to the house, and it'll be quick."

CHAPTER 3

A little while later, later Mike and Billy were walking through the office of the second in charge at MMC, Tyler Garrett. "Good to see you, Tyler. You keeping the place running?"

"I sure am, boss man. Glad you made it to town in one piece. How do you like the weather?"

"Oh man, it's hot! And no air-conditioning at our house—got a window box, but it doesn't seem to make a bit of difference." He turned toward Billy. "Tyler, I'd like you to meet my son Billy. He's sixteen and will be a junior at the high school next year." They shook hands.

"Great to meet you, Billy. You look like your old man."

"Thanks, I guess," said Billy.

"Oh come on, you'll do well if you look like me," Mike said. He turned back to Tyler. "I'll be starting next week. Just got to get situated here first. We stopped by the school to get Billy enrolled this morning."

"Yeah, how was that?"

"Fine. Got his classes and met the football coach. What a character he is."

"What do you mean?"

"Oh, just a tough guy type. Lots of swagger."

"That's Coach Logan, all right."

"He said something I can't figure out, though. He said MMC was the *second*-biggest thing in town. Aren't we the biggest employer here?"

"We sure are," Tyler confirmed. "Twelve hundred and sixty-one people as of last week's payroll."

"Then what does he mean by us being the second-biggest thing? I don't get it?"

"He didn't tell you?"

"No. He said he wouldn't do my work for me or something like that. Do you know what he's talking about?"

"Of course I do. Everybody does. Well, except you. But that won't take you but a day or two to figure out."

"For goodness' sake, why all the mystery? Just tell me what it is that's the 'biggest thing in East Creek'!"

"Aw, no way. Too much fun seeing you all bugged out by it. But I will give you a hint."

"Okay . . ."

"What door did you use to get into Coach's building?"

"The one to the locker room," Billy chimed in.

"That explains it, then. Next time you go back, you go in through the main foyer door. That will explain everything."

"What? What do they have, some sort of famous mural or something? An autographed football from Roger Staubach? What?"

"Just see for yourself, Mike." Just then the office phone rang. Tyler told Mike he had to take it. Mike confirmed he would be in next Monday at nine and he and Billy cut out through a side exit directly to their car in the parking lot.

CHAPTER 4

After two days of unpacking and ordering pizza in, Mike and Billy headed out to the small mall in town to look for back-to-school clothes and some gear Billy would need for football. On the way home, Mike suggested they stop at the burger stand and get some ice cream. Billy readily agreed. As they drove past the high school, Mike made a sudden turn into the gym parking lot.

"What are you doing, Dad?"

"I gotta check something out. It's been bugging me for days." He pulled into a parking spot close to the gym. There was a smattering of other cars in the lot but not too many people at the school. *Probably just the janitor and some coaching staff around today*, Mike thought.

"What's been bugging you?"

"Everybody talking about the 'biggest thing in town' in the foyer of this gym. I can't imagine what it is." He opened his door. "Come on. Let's see."

They walked up the stairs and pulled open the door to the foyer of the gymnasium. It took Mike less than a second to see what the biggest thing in town was. He and Billy walked slowly toward the glass case that stretched some seventy-five feet along the wall.

"Wow," Billy said.

"I'll say wow," Mike agreed.

"How many are there?"

"Well, let's count." They started at the left side and moved right. "One, two, three . . . ten, eleven, twelve . . . sixteen, seventeen. *Seventeen*."

"Wow," Billy repeated.

"You said that already," Mike said as he laughed.

There before them, amidst a lot of other memorabilia, sat the shiny proof of the biggest thing in East Creek, Texas.

Seventeen Golden Football trophies. At the bottom of each was inscribed:

Texas State High School Football Champions

East Creek Cougars

Coach Brock Logan

The only thing different from trophy to trophy was the year engraved on each. The two of them

24

looked back through the trophies and realized that in the last twenty-six years, Coach Brock Logan and the East Creek Cougars had won seventeen State High School Football Championships.

"That's almost seventy percent," Billy noted.

"Indeed it is. Most coaches would be happy with a seventy percent win-loss ratio. This guy has a seventy-thirty *State Championship* ratio!"

They spent the next ten minutes looking through the pictures and jerseys and autographed footballs in the case. They noted especially the pictures of a much younger Brock Logan and even a few players who had gone on to play in the National Football League.

On the way home they stopped and grabbed burgers and ice cream, talking about the football program at East Creek. Billy was even more excited about playing and it was taking some of the edge off of his lack of desire to be in Texas rather than Illinois.

CHAPTER 5

"Howdy, neighbor," a cheery feminine voice sang out of nowhere.

Mike looked up from the ribs he was cooking on the grill and stared around. Sticking above the side fence was a head that obviously went with the voice: attractive, about forty, blond. Big hair, but not *big* hair like so many think of in Texas. He put the grill tools down and wandered closer to the fence.

"Sorry I haven't been over to welcome you," the woman continued, "but I just got back from a trip and noticed somebody had moved in. I normally bring cookies or a pie over when someone moves into the neighborhood. So, yeah. Sorry." She paused. "My name's Tanya, by the way. Tanya Knoll. I, uh . . . I live next door to you."

"I sorta figured," Mike said. By now he was close enough to the fence to have to crane his neck.

"Either that or my real neighbors would be upset with a woman yelling over their fence." He smiled.

"Oh, yeah. Well. I saw the smoke from your grill and thought I would pop my head up. I hope that's okay."

"Sure, no problem. Nice to meet you, Tanya. I'm Mike." He reached his hand up as she reached her hand down over the fence. They shook on their new neighbor status.

"So, is there a Mr. Tanya?"

"Nope. Not anymore, unfortunately. Well, I take that back. He was a rascal. Always runnin' around, drinking, playin' pool till all hours of the morning. I don't know. It's a long story. What about you? Is there a Mrs. Mike?"

"There is a Mrs. Mike. But she lives in Chicago where we came from."

"Why does she live in Chicago?"

"She's trying to decide if she wants to continue to be Mrs. Mike."

"Oh sweetie, that's too bad. She'll come around, I'm sure."

"Well, we'll see about that. I hope she does."

"You said 'we.' Who is we? You got kids?"

"I do. Billy. He's a junior this year."

"Oooh, I bet he's a football player, isn't he? Football, you know, that's the biggest thing here in East Creek. Bigger even than the Markston Machine plant."

"So I've heard."

"What do you for work, Mike?"

"Tanya, I *run* the second-biggest thing in East Creek." He liked the sound of that. "Markston Machine. I'm the new plant manager."

She tilted her head back and laughed. "Oh sure, I heard the new guy was coming to town to take over for old man Jones. I should've known."

Mike was beginning to think that Tanya was a bit . . . flighty. That was the word he was looking for. "And what do *you* do for a living, Tanya?"

"Me? I'm a legal secretary. I know *secretary* isn't politically correct anymore, but I don't care. I'm a secretary. Larry, my boss, he's a one-man shop. He says he is a *personal injury attorney*. I know, I know. He's an ambulance chaser. He'll admit it if you put a couple of gin and tonics in him. But he prefers the more legit term. That's a lawyer for you, right?"

Man, she can talk. He could tell she was a good person, though. Oddly, he liked her. And, considering he and Billy knew virtually no one here, it was nice to have a good neighbor.

"What are you standing on?" he asked.

"What?"

"Standing on. What are you standing on? To look over the fence. It's got to be too tall for you to just be standing there."

"Oh, yeah. It's a bucket, on a footstool, on a table. It's safe though. I'm good with balance. I did gymnastics when I was a kid. That is, until Daddy died and Momma couldn't afford the lessons anymore. Then they stopped doing it in high school because of the insurance costs run up by people like, well, like my boss Larry."

Mike looked back at the grill. He figured Tanya looked skinny so she probably wouldn't eat much. He was sure they had enough food for a third person. "Well, Tanya, you aren't a vegetarian, are you?"

"Me. No way. Mike, this is Texas. We love us some beef." Her face suddenly lit up. "You're inviting me over for dinner, aren't you? Look at you. You're a great neighbor. I should be the one inviting *you* over. Okay, I'll be right over. This will be great. I'll bring a salad. I have salad. See you in a few minutes." With that, her head disappeared. Mike heard what sounded like a bucket falling off a footstool falling off a table, ending with a dull thud on the ground. The words came from over the fence, "I'm okay. It's okay. See you in a few minutes!"

"Yep," Mike said to no one in particular. "I'm inviting you over. See you in a few minutes."

As he turned and walked back to the grill he thought, *This will be interesting*.

After dinner Mike and Billy cleaned up the table winding up in the kitchen together while Tanya sat out on the back deck. "Man, Dad, that lady can *talk*."

"Yes she can. That she can. She's interesting, though."

"And funny. What a crack-up some of the stories. Except she takes *way* too long to tell them."

"I actually found that to be the funny part after a while."

"Yeah, I guess so."

"So son, you going to join us out back for a little longer or do you have video games to play?"

"Video games. Have fun listening to stories." With that Billy turned and went down the hall.

Mike popped his head out the sliding glass door and asked if Tanya would like anything else to drink.

"Nope. I still have some of this delicious lemonade you made." The night was beginning to cool off a bit. "So, Mike, are you here for the duration?"

"No. No offense, Tanya, but I don't hope to be here very long at all. I want to get back up to Chicago. I'm a city boy."

"Yeah, the loafers with the black socks and the khaki shorts gave it away," she said with a smile.

"What are you talking about? This is a great look!"

"Uh-huh. You need some cowboy boots. Just sayin'."

Mike decided to change the subject back. "Anyway, I want to get back to Chicago. Maybe I can get my wife to take me back."

"What's her name?"

"Kristy."

"That's a nice name. I had a friend named Kristy once. She moved away in the seventh grade though. Never did find out what happened to her. Just up and moved."

They sat quiet for a few moments.

"So, why did Kristy kick you out?"

"How do you know she kicked me out?"

"The way you talk. You wouldn't want her to take you back if you left yourself."

"Oh, it's a long story. I think she just realized I wasn't going to become the person she wanted to be married to. Maybe she took a risk when we got married."

"What do you mean a risk?"

"Well, people always talked about my potential. Heck, I thought I had potential. Then you wake up twenty years later, your wife has kicked you out and you're living in East Creek, Texas. No offense."

"Oh, I know what you mean. Well, maybe you're here to learn something. I am a *big believer* in that kind of stuff. Nothing happens by happenstance. It all happens for a purpose."

"Yeah, maybe."

"Not maybe. *That's* why you and Billy are here, I bet. You have something to learn."

"Yeah, East Creek, Texas, bastion of higher education."

"All right, I'll take one shot about East Creek, but if you keep talking that way, I won't take it. East Creek may not be the big city and all, but the people here are good folks, and you could learn a lot from them. You just have to decide to."

"I guess . . ." Mike took another gulp of lemonade.

"So, your job is to look for what you are going to learn. And then apply it. You know, I have been reading self-help books for years. That's what they teach you: Learn it. Apply it. What are you going to learn so you can apply it?"

"I don't know, Tanya. I didn't invite you over to hear a motivational speech."

"Well maybe you need one. Seems to me like you're the one who's lost. I *choose* to live here."

Ouch. That hurt. But Mike got it. "Okay, I'll keep an open mind."

"Good. And what do you hope happens?"

"My goal?"

"Or goals?"

"Well the obvious: Get my wife back and get out of East Creek."

"Simple enough. I'll help you. I can be a good sounding board. And I can motivate you too. Nothing like having a neighbor with energy. And energy I have by the truckload."

"That you do, Tanya. That you do. Okay, I'll get my wife back and get back to Chicago. That's the goal, and you can be my personal motivator. Deal?"

"Deal, neighbor."

CHAPTER 6

ike and Billy arrived at the football field Monday morning at four o'clock sharp. Practice, according to Billy's letter from Coach Logan, started at 4:30 AM. The parking lot was full, and lots of high school kids were coming in already.

"Four AM. Wow. Practice never started this early in Chicago."

"No, son, but it sounds like they take it seriously here. Or, more seriously."

The letter had also called for at least one parent to be at the opening of practice the first day so the coach could address them, so a lot of cars were sitting in the lot with just a parent waiting for the practice to start. Around 4:25 they all wandered over to the field and sat in the bleachers. At 4:30 exactly, the locker room door burst open and out came the team. Mike noticed immediately that they were all neatly in line and in sync. They took one lap around the field, led by Coach Logan himself, and then came to rest in front of the parents. The boys all dropped to one knee and listened as Coach Logan talked.

"Good morning, parents. I am Coach Logan, and this is this year's Cougar football team, the next Texas State Champions!" The small group of parents made a pretty good noise for so early in the morning. "I am thankful that you have entrusted them to me. I promise that I will make them into the best ball players they can be. More than that, I will make them into men. They will be the best students they can be and they will develop character and become leaders. That is my most important task for this year. Now, if there are no questions, we have a long year ahead and we need to get started. I appreciate you seeing to your boys getting here this morning." He turned to the young players and shouted, "Hit the field!" With that, they all took off and formed a square formation at the twenty-yard line. "Parents, if you have any questions or concerns, please let me know." Coach Logan turned and jogged out to join his players.

Mike turned to a man sitting next to him. "Hey there," he said extending his hand. "I'm Mike Keller."

"John Carter," the man said as they shook hands.

"We're new to town. Just moved here from Chicago. My boy Billy is a junior."

"Chicago, huh? What brought you here?"

"MMC. I'm the new head of the plant."

"I heard they got a new guy. You're it?"

"Yep. I'm excited to get going."

"Well, they need some new leadership. I hope you're up to it."

"I think I am. But I could always become a better leader myself."

"Well, you ought to spend some time with Coach Logan, then. He's the best leader I've ever met."

"Really? I mean, he's won a bunch of championships, but he's a . . . just a football coach."

"First of all, some advice. Don't *ever* let anyone hear you say that around here again. Talkin' against Coach Logan would be your death knell. Secondly, wait until you get to know him. If Coach Logan were in the military, he'd be a general. If he were in business, he'd be the CEO. If he were in politics, he'd be the president. As it is, he's in high school football and he is the winningest football coach in the history of the greatest football state in the nation. He's that good."

"Really? I guess I have a lot to learn. So how could I get to know him?"

"Volunteer to help him watch tape."

"Watch tape?"

"Yeah, he and the coaches watch game and practice video to pick things up that will help them for future games. He takes a few volunteers every year. It's hard to get a spot, but being you're so high up at MMC I bet he'd let you in. They watch it every night, but you could volunteer on Tuesday nights. That's their important one for the week. Check with him. There is no one better you could learn leadership from."

"Thanks, John, I will do that. Should I just call and ask him?"

"That would do it, if he lets you in."

CHAPTER 7

Mike and Billy were sitting in front of the television late Wednesday night when the phone rang. Mike grabbed it. "Hello."

"Mike?"

"This is he."

"Coach Logan here."

"Oh, hey, Coach Logan. Thanks for the return call."

"No problem. I got your message. I am very selective about who we have as our volunteers, but I'll take a chance on you since you're the head guy at MMC. You must be good at what you do. Do you know anything about football?"

"Well, I'm not Vince Lombardi, but I played growing up and am a big fan. I won my fantasy football league championship one year." As soon as he said that, he knew it was a disaster.

"Fantasy football league?"

"Yeah, I mean . . ."

"Right. Well, I'll let you volunteer in spite of that. There's nothing fantasy about what we're doing here, Mike."

"I know, I shouldn't have, uh . . ."

"Look, Mike, I've been watchin' your boy. He's pretty good. It's hard for someone to move in here his junior year, but we have a spot or two that I could see him getting some time in. Now, I'm not promising anything, but Billy works hard, hits hard, and seems to have a good mind. That's what we look for. I think he could see some action."

"Wow, that's great. I'll tell him."

"No, don't tell him. He still has a long way to go and needs to keep workin' at it. He's on the right track, though."

"Oh, okay. So when do you need me?"

"Well, first game is three weeks out. I'll have you in for our Tuesday night sessions, but we have a get-together this Friday you need to be at. My house. Burgers, ribs, and dogs. No need to bring anything. Just be here at seven sharp. We'll eat and then watch some tape. It'll give you a chance to meet some of the other coaches and see how we do things. Four-eleven Oak Street. I'll see you then."

"Okay, Coach." The line was already dead. *I'm a grown man. I can't believe I just called a guy "Coach."*

CHAPTER 8

Mike decided to try to get to practice Thursday and Friday, at least for the tail end, so he could get a feel for how it went. He also wanted to see Billy in action. What he saw reminded him of a military exercise. He'd never seen high school kids stretched so far. It actually made him a bit uncomfortable, even though the kids seemed to respond and handled it well. He figured he could ask about it at the Friday night meeting with Coach Logan.

The barbeque came quick enough. Mike found himself, beer in hand, with a group of men he'd never met before—all standing around the grill watching meat cook. All the talk was football. Every time Mike introduced himself there would be a conversation about how the plant needed new leadership and then quickly back to football. Mike was talking more about football and leadership than he ever had before. The football part made sense, but all the talk about leadership surprised him.

Eventually everyone got their plates full and they all sat in a circle out in Coach Logan's backyard.

"So, we'll get to tape after dinner. Now's the time to talk about whatever you guys want to talk about. What's the topic?" Everyone looked around to see who would be the first to bring something up. After a few moments, Mike decided it would be him.

"I have a question. Now, I know I'm the new guy here, so I'm just trying to get to know the program. It seems to me like you work these kids pretty hard and set the bar pretty high. I'm all for pushing the kids, but do you think it may be too hard?"

Time stopped. Everyone sat, mouth open, staring at him. Total silence. It was obvious that this was a question that had never been asked before. Probably never even thought before. *By the looks on their faces*, Mike thought, *you would have thought I suggested we all strip down and run naked through downtown East Creek.* After an awkward moment, Coach Logan graciously broke the silence.

"That's a good question, Mike. And an important issue. Happy to deal with it." The other men looked at Coach Logan. Mike felt like he was being brought back slowly from the brink. *Maybe I should have kept my mouth shut.* "Mike, as you settle in here, you're going to find that one thing is more important to me than football, and that's leadership. Ultimately, I am building leaders. Some of these young men will go to college and play football there. A very few will go on to the NFL." He turned to Carl Connors. "Carl, how many of our kids have played in the NFL?"

"Seven," Carl answered.

Coach Logan turned back to Mike. "Seven. That's good for a high school, I suppose, but it is a very low percentage. Of the seven, two had a career out of it. You see, this isn't really about football. It's about leadership. All of these young men will go on to build businesses, raise families, and the like. The long-term goal isn't about winning championships. It's about *making champions*. And champions are leaders. Every single kid who comes through our program can be a leader in life. That's what we're about here.

"So, to answer your question directly. My first rule of leadership is this: *You get what you expect.* Do I push these kids hard? Yep. Probably harder than they will be pushed ever again in their lives. Does that hurt them? Of course not. Mike, as I see it, most leaders set the bar too low. People don't respond to low expectations. They respond to high expectations. What do you suppose I would get out of my team if I started every year telling them I hoped we could make the playoffs?"

"Uh, I guess they would shoot for that."

"That's right. That's exactly what they would shoot for. They might hope for more, but they would aim for the playoffs. So instead, I tell them I expect to win the state championship. That is the expectation."

"Okay, I get that. That's the goal. But as hard as we push them in practice . . ."

"Mike, here's the problem with teenagers, and people in general: No one expects anything of them. Everyone expects teenagers to be lazy, sleep in, cut class, party, and play video games. And what do they do? They become lazy, sleep in, cut class, party, and play video games. And when they grow up, what do we expect of them?

To be average. That's why most people end up average. Well, I'll let other coaches produce thousands of average people. The Cougar program is designed to produce leaders. We're a leader-makin' machine, aren't we, boys?" The rest of the men agreed.

Phil Burns said it best. "We makin' us some flat out leaders all right. Flat. Out." Then he tipped back another slug of beer.

"Mike, here's what I expect: I expect them to be the best students they can be. I expect them to be honorable young men. I expect them to treat their elders with respect. I expect them to be on time. I expect them to be prepared. I expect them to give a hundred and ten percent every single moment they are on the field. I expect every one of them to be a selfless team player. And I expect them to play to win every single game. That isn't what we hope for. That's what we *expect*."

"That's certainly great, Coach, but isn't that what everyone expects?"

"No, Mike, it isn't. They may pay lip service to it, but we mean it. You're right in that every coach says the same thing, but we not only say it, we demand it. Thousands, tens of thousands of coaches say they expect the best from their players, but then they accept less than that. We don't accept anything less than what we expect."

"Isn't that a bit unrealistic?"

"Is it? I got a truckload of golden hardware in that gym—seventeen state championship trophies—to say it isn't unrealistic at all. The difference is accountability. We hold people accountable to what the team expectations are. Here's an example. Chuck Gillan. Ever heard of him?" Around the circle, heads nodded knowingly.

"No."

"Too bad. He could've been an NFL quarterback. Guess what he's doin' now? Slinging a broom at a grain elevator. You know why?"

"Why?"

"Chuck was the best quarterback ever to come through here. Probably one of the top three QBs in Texas history. We called him 'Gunner.' Had a rocket launcher for an arm. Sixteen years old he's throwing forty yards down and out on a rope." One of the other guys in the circle, Baxter Murphy, looked to the sky and whistled, obviously remembering a pass Gunner had thrown. Coach turned to him. "You thinking about his first freshman game?"

"Yep." Baxter turned to Mike, eyes lit up. "We're down by six with ten seconds left against a big-time city program. Our Senior QB had broken his arm in the third quarter. In comes Gunner. He was kind of a secret weapon at that point, so they didn't have a read on him. They're in a Prevent Defense. It is obvious we have to go for the end zone. Most people would lob it up and hope for the best. Coach calls for one of our receivers to run a buttonhook at the front right of the end zone, maybe one yard deep. This is a throw most pros wouldn't try. Gunner lets go with one of the best passes in high school history. Threads it between three guys, right into the hands of his wide out. TD, we win. Wow, he was somethin'."

"And then the bottom fell out," Coach said.

"What happened?" Mike asked.

"Well, like I said, we have expectations and we hold people accountable to them. This kid had the world by the tail, but he wouldn't follow the rules. Thought he was better than everyone else. He would show up late for practice, dog it through

51

exercises, do poorly in class, go out drinkin' after the games. It just wasn't acceptable."

"That sounds like a lot of high schoolers, doesn't it?"

"It sounds like a lot of high school kids who don't know how to win. Don't know how to set their sights on a goal far beyond themselves and then execute the achievement of that goal. That's why the East Creek Cougars are workin' on state championship number eighteen this year."

"So what happened to Gunner? What did you do?"

"I sat him. It killed me. Never in my life before or since did I want to break one of my own rules like I did with Gunner. I was lookin' for a reason to let him play. I just couldn't do it. Not for me, and not for my kids. I put him on the bench. I thought that might light a fire under him. It didn't. Eventually I kicked him off the team for being a distraction. He dropped out of school his junior year. Moved to Nebraska to live with a cousin. Last I heard he was makin' eight bucks an hour."

"Well, that must have been a bummer for that year, huh?"

"Oh no, we won state that year. Had a kid who was a junior who was our number three QB. He stepped in, became a leader, and away we went. Didn't have a great passing game that year, but we had a strong ground game and a heckuva defense. Won twenty-one–twenty in Texas Stadium. It was a sweet victory. We proved you can stick to your values and still win. It was a great lesson about leadership for me, the staff, and the team. And guess where that QB is now?"

"Where?"

"He started a business up in Oklahoma doin' twenty million a year. Became a real leader, that kid."

"So, you get what you expect?"

"You get what you expect, and what you hold people accountable for. This ain't rocket science, Mike."

"Sounds simple enough."

"You know, so many people try to make it rocket science. It ain't rocket science. I have a few other leadership rules. I'll teach 'em to ya. In the meantime, let's go watch some tape."

Everyone jumped up and started moving to the house. It was time for some football.

CHAPTER 9

S unday afternoon was quiet and lazy until the doorbell rang. Mike opened the door and saw Tanya standing there, a huge platter in her hands, the contents hidden by foil. "Howdy, neighbor!"

"Hi, Tanya. Come on in." Stepping aside, he waved her in. "What do you have there?"

"These are my *world famous* cookies. Chocolate chip and oatmeal. They are out of this world and since you moved in I've felt so guilty that I haven't given you a proper welcome gift." She walked past Mike and straight for the kitchen. "These are fresh out of the oven. You and Billy are going to love them. They aren't really *world famous* but they are very good. They are the hit of every family reunion." She tore the foil off and the smell wafted through the kitchen. That was enough for Mike. He grabbed one in each hand and took a bite.

"Wow, these are amazing."

"Told ya. People love 'em."

"I can see why . . . Hey, Tanya, you got a few minutes?"

"Sure, what's up? Sounds serious."

"I've been thinking about something and wanted to run it by you. Let me get you some iced tea and we can sit out back."

A few moments later they were sitting on the deck. "So Tanya, what do you know about Brock Logan?"

"Coach? A lot. I grew up two doors down from him. We were in the same grade. In fact, if you don't tell anyone, he was my first crush. Sixth grade. He was sooo cute."

"Wow, sorry I asked," Mike said with a smile.

"Oh you . . . Yep, I've known him for ever. Why, what do you want to know about him?"

"Let's start with what his story is."

"Pretty simple, really. He grew up here. Average student. Maybe a little above average. He wrestled and played football."

"Football star?"

"Nope. Nobody ever would have guessed he'd become the greatest high school football coach in Texas history."

"Really? So how'd that happen?"

"He went off to the Army. Gave it four years, then came back to town and got a job at MMC. The high school needed a football coach and no one wanted the job. It just wasn't big back then. He is a self-made man. He figured something out about life and he figured out how to teach it to others. Turned that team around—and I guess, as they say, 'The rest is history.'"

"What do you know about these *leadership rules* he talks about?"

"I've heard of them. I don't know what they are. That's his big thing, I know, leadership." Tanya got up and moved toward the kitchen. "Want another cookie? I'm going to get some."

"Sure, grab me a couple."

When she was back outside, she asked, "So, how's Kristy?"

"Huh? What?" Mike was taken aback.

"You know, Mrs. Mike. What's happening there?"

"Oh, I talked to her the other day. It's fine."

"Really?"

"Well, I mean, we're working on it. I don't know . . ."

"What do you think she thinks you want?"

57

"I don't know." He took a sip of his iced tea.

"She is probably wondering whether you want it to work or not. You have to let her know you want it to work. You have to work at it. What do you want to happen? You know, you get what you expect."

Mike's head snapped around. "What did you say?"

"What do you want to happen?"

"No, after that."

"I don't know. What are you talking about?"

"Did you say, 'You get what you expect'?"

"Oh, yeah. I say that all the time. It's true. *You get what you expect.* What's wrong with that?"

Mike looked away. "Nothing wrong with it. Just interesting, that's all. I heard it somewhere else the other day. Coach Logan said that to me."

"Great minds think alike, right?" She smiled.

CHAPTER 10

S aturday afternoon Billy had one of his new friends, a kid named Allan, over to play the new Madden football video game. Allan also played football but didn't get much action in games. A little too small. He was smart, though, and he and Billy had a few classes together.

They talked while they went back and forth on the big screen TV. "So, how do you like East Creek?" Allan asked.

"It's all right. Hotter than anyplace I've ever been in before."

"It won't be that bad for long. And at least your dad bought you air-conditioning." Allan threw a virtual pass for a touchdown and jumped up and down celebrating. During setup for the next kickoff he asked, "You miss your mom?"

"Huh?" Billy was taken aback. He didn't normally talk about his family problems with others. He barely ever talked about them with his own parents.

"I mean, do you miss her?"

"Yeah, I guess so."

"What did your dad do that was so bad that she kicked you guys out?"

Billy dropped the controls. "He didn't do anything. What's your problem, anyway? Why do you want to know all this stuff?"

"Hey dude, I'm not trying to cause a problem. Just thought you might want to talk about it. Can't be fun moving across the country to East Creek and leaving your mom behind."

Billy received the kickoff and ran it back thirty-five yards. "Well, I'm just a little sensitive about it. I don't like talking about it. But I'll tell you if you want to know."

"Sure, if you want to tell me. But you don't have to."

"Nah, it's okay." They paused the game. "My mom and dad are both really high achievers. At least they want to be. My mom always talks about my dad's potential. And then, he hit this wall at work. They had always talked about him becoming CEO, making all this money, vacation homes, whatever. I heard them arguing one night. Dad just wasn't going very fast. I think they overspent the money. It kinda all went downhill from there."

"Your mom dumped your dad because he didn't get a promotion? That's harsh."

"No, that's not it. That was what happened, but she always complained that he wasn't growing anymore. She was always saying that he gave up and was just coasting. Thought the world owed him something on a silver platter."

"Is that right?"

"No. I don't think so. My dad's cool. I don't really know what the problem is, though. I guess my mom wanted my dad to become something else and he wouldn't change or something. That's about all I get."

"So, do you miss her?"

"Yeah. I miss her. I hope they get back together."

"Well, maybe they will." Not much else to say at that point. They went back to playing Madden.

CHAPTER 11

M ike blew into MMC around 9:45 AM and went straight to Tyler's office. "Hey Tyler, how was the weekend?"

"Pretty good, boss. How about yours?"

"Great. Back to work." He sat down across from Tyler. "Hey, I've been thinking about something. Maybe we don't expect enough out of our employees."

"What do you mean?"

"Well, you know, most of them come to work here and stay a long time. There isn't much room for advancement. I think a lot of them just sort of settle into the status quo. Our work suffers and we don't get the most out of them. So we need to expect more."

"Where is all this coming from?"

"Coach Logan. I'm helping out with the video review of games and practices. We got to talking about it."

"So you want to run MMC like a high school football team?"

"No, of course not. I mean, well, maybe. Not like a football team per se, but Coach Logan made a lot of sense about how he sets high expectations for the players and they rise to it. Maybe that's something we should focus on here."

"Well, the grumble about old man Jones—and believe me, I agree—is that he just settled in here and let it all run on autopilot. People are definitely comfortable here. They check in, do their job, check out, and go home."

"We're going to change that."

"All right, what do you propose?"

"You and I could work on it. Maybe bring in a few like-minded folks and set up some clear goals and set employee expectations for their work. What do you think?"

"I'm game. Just let me know what you want me to do."

"Get me a list of any go-getters we have. Or people you think could be. Make sure that we get a cross-section of people from top to bottom so we get a good idea of what people are thinking across the board. We'll get them in a room and spend a few hours with them."

"Will do, boss."

The next two weeks, Mike and Tyler and eighteen other people, hand-picked from the plant, worked together to set expectations for employee values, attitudes, and behavior. They met for hours at a time talking about what people's current mindsets were, what they should be, and how to get them there. When they had finally hammered out a document that represented not only the goals of the corporate office but also the ideas of the East Creek workers, they rolled it out through the plant.

It wasn't exactly well received. Most of the people who worked at MMC had done so for years. In East Creek, once you got in with MMC you stayed there. The pay was fine, the benefits were the best in town, and once you were off shift, you were done for the day. No taking work home for any of them. For the most part, people were pretty complacent at work, never striving for more than was considered average. But then again, that was all that was expected of them.

They weren't ever expected to pursue excellence at work, and they certainly were never expected to think about MMC outside of work.

The lack of change bothered Mike. For him, it was a struggle to motivate his people. He had never really faced a group mindset anything like the one at the MMC plant. He pushed, and people pushed back. He got frustrated with what he felt was his own lack of ability to lead and the people's lack of desire to follow and change. He decided to get some advice.

"Door's open!"

Mike pushed Coach Logan's on door and walked in.

"Mike, how's it goin'?"

"Pretty good, Coach. You got a minute?"

"Sure. I got about fifteen minutes. What's up?"

"Well, I feel kind of foolish coming in here asking for advice and all, but . . ." His voice trailed off.

"Well, I know you ain't no fool."

"It's just, you know. I'm a highly educated executive. I should know what I'm doing—"

"And I'm just a high school football coach?"

"I don't mean it that way."

"Sure you do. I'm good with that, though."

"You are?"

"Sure. Because I know better. I don't buy into society's pecking order. CEOs at the top, high school football coaches at the bottom. It's bogus."

"Well, that's a good perspective, I guess."

"Mike, it isn't a perspective. It's a reality. You're the one coming to me, remember?"

"Sure, but—"

"But nothing. You grab any CEO off the street and ask him if he'd like to win seventeen Texas State high school football championships, get the Gatorade shower, and get carried off the field by fifty screaming young champions who just proved to themselves that yes, anything is possible if they strive for it, and every single one of them would change places with me in a heartbeat. No second thoughts at all. Any leader would love to have the success I've had. I don't care that I only make $40,000 a year. I win. I make a difference. I change lives. That's all that matters. I'm not trying to keep up with the big boys in the monkey suits and I have nothing to prove. I am what I am and I'm happy with it.

"But what I find funny is how you guys are all out comparing yourselves with yourselves. You're all afraid to fail. You all want to be great leaders but you don't actually lead. You have thousands of books on leadership. Weekend seminars. Fancy degrees in it. Now don't get me wrong. Those things are fine, but we've made it *way too complex*. Most leadership is *simple*. Simple, Mike. Make it simple. Don't overthink. You follow a few rules, like the one I told you a few weeks back, and you'll fix most of your leadership problems." He paused. Mike just sat there. "So, what's the problem?"

Mike leaned forward. "Well, I guess I never thought of it that way. Let me think for a minute . . . I really thought about what you said that night at your house, that *you get what you expect*. I like that. I have tried to implement that at MMC. We got some of the leaders together and set it all out: What we want their attitudes to be, what expected behavior is. All that stuff."

"And?"

"And it isn't working."

"Gotcha."

"What do I do?"

"Here's your problem. This is going to be a long-term change. These folks have worked this way for *decades*. It's good you want to change, and it will happen. It took me a few years to get the Cougar program turned around. It helped that I got some wins the first year. They hadn't won much before that. But it took awhile. So you are right to change expectations. Now, here's a question for ya: Do you follow the expectations you set for the people you lead?"

"What?"

"You heard me. Do you follow the expectations you set for others? Do you do what you tell them to do? This here is my second rule of leadership: *You get what you model.*"

"I don't know that it's that simple, Coach."

"That's the problem with you fancy-pants city slickers."

Mike looked at his pants then back at the coach. "What's that supposed to mean?"

"Mike, I'm a straight shooter. So I'm gonna shoot straight with you. You college-educated guys can be so brainless sometimes. Not that college is bad. I try to get all my players to go. It just amazes me that so many people can spend a hundred thousand bucks on learnin' and have no understanding about how things really work. Mike, here's the fact: You can't tell your people to do something that you won't do yourself. You can come up with all sorts of mission statements, values charts, lists of expectations that everyone is supposed to follow, but ultimately, they are looking at you, the leader, to see what they are supposed to do. So, one more time: Do you do what you tell them to do?"

Mike sat back in his chair. Lots of little things flooded his mind. "Well, I do for the most part."

"Not good enough. Think, Mike. What do you tell them to do that you don't do yourself?"

"I don't know. I . . ."

"Sure you do, Mike. Look, I'm not a counselor. I don't need to give you a shoulder to cry on. You came here lookin' for advice and I'm willing to give it to you. But I'm not gonna play games with you and do this dance. Now, answer the question. Be honest with yourself."

"We expect them to be at work at eight."

"And . . . ?"

"That isn't what I do. I come in later."

"Later?"

"Nine or nine-thirty. I've actually heard some people grumbling about it."

"What else have you heard grumbling about?"

"Leaving early. A bad attitude . . . "

"A bad attitude? They say you have a bad attitude?"

"Yeah. We came out with the expectation of demonstrating a positive attitude at all times and I guess I don't."

"That's a deal killer. You expect them to stay and act positive and you don't. Why?"

"Look, Coach, I don't like the fact that I'm here in East Creek. I was moving along in Chicago. I had lots of responsibility. I was making great money living in a world-class city, and now here I am in Podunk Texas working with people who settled for average thirty years ago." Mike surprised himself with how blunt it came out.

"Poor Mike. Poor, poor Mike. You have it so tough." Mike just stared at Coach Logan. "You know what will make you successful in Chicago?"

"What?"

71

"If you are successful here. I'm guessing the big shots back in Chicago weren't happy with your work and that's why you're here in Texas. Nothin' you can do about that. Now, you can sit around and cry in your pity party, or you can suck it up and become a leader. A *real* leader. Real leaders set expectations for the group and then they *lead* by modeling those expectations. You can't deal in theory. Telling others to do something and not doing it yourself ain't leadership.

"Now, I like it here in East Creek. It's a great place. But I get that you don't like it. But you got bigger problems than living in—what did you call it—Podunk? If you don't do a good job here, your next stop is a third-world plant, not back to Chicago. Your choice. And your biggest problem is that you aren't a leader in your family."

"What? Where did that come from?"

"Billy talked to me about what's going on with you and his mother. Mike, I like you. You're a good guy. You're just lost, that's all. But you have potential. You need to learn this stuff and take the MMC plant here to the next level. And you need to get your wife back by being a leader. That's the only way to get back to Chicago."

"But there's a big difference between leading MMC and what I need to do with my wife and family . . . Isn't there?"

"Sure, they're different in a lot of ways, but here's something we 'uneducated' folks know: *People's people.* Doesn't matter how old, where they're from. Nothin'. If you want them to follow you, you need to know that *You get what you expect* and *You get what you model.* People are looking for someone to take them to a better place and who will lead the way by example. That's true in a family, on a sports team, or in a big company. Basic leadership, that's what that is."

That's a lot to think about—that's for sure. Mike found it hard enough to realize he had to raise his expectations, but harder still to implement those expectations in his own life so he could be an authentic leader. That was now task one: Start living what he expected others to live.

Tanya answered on the third ring. "Hello?"

"Tanya, it's Mike, next door."

"Hey, Mike, that is so weird. I was just thinking about you. Actually I was sitting doing my nails so I was thinking about that but I *had* thought about you a minute ago. By the way, I have wet nails, so if I drop the receiver, just wait until I pick up the phone again."

"Tanya?"

"Yeah, I'm here."

"I know you're there. Just quit talking for a minute."

She laughed. This wasn't the first time she'd ever heard that. "Okay, sorry. What can I do for you, Mike?"

"Look, I've been talking to Coach Logan again and I want to run something by you . . . since you're a girl."

"You've been talking to Coach Logan about *girls?*"

"No, I was talking to him about leadership. I'm trying to turn MMC around and Coach Logan knows a lot about leadership—so I was talking to him about that."

"So why are you calling me to talk about girls? Maybe I'm missing something."

"No, you aren't missing anything. Here's the deal. Coach was telling me that, basically, I have to practice what I preach."

"Well, that's good advice. I concur. I love that word 'concur.' My boss uses it all the time."

"Tanya, focus."

"Sorry."

"So, here's why I need a girl's advice. I need to work harder at getting Kristy back."

"Oh, that's so romantic! And you want me to help? I could totally help!"

"Let's start with some advice. I know now that I was never really a good example either to Kristy or to Billy. It makes sense that she had a hard time respecting me. But how do I get that back? What can I do now?"

"Oh, I get it. I think you need to take the direct approach. And apologize."

"Won't that make me look weak?"

"No, a man who takes responsibility isn't weak. That's strong. That's the way to start over. Tell her you're sorry and that you know what to do now. Then start doing it."

"I don't know if it's that simple."

"What other options do you have?"

"You're right. All right, I'll call her."

"You're a good man, Mike."

"Thanks, Tanya. I gotta go."

"Bye."

Mike hung up the phone and then just stared at it. Mike hadn't remembered ever being so nervous about talking to Kristy. At least not since before they were married. He knew he had to call her, though. Tanya was right. He had to try to push the reset button, and that started with him owning up to his own behavior.

He dialed the number and waited. Kristy answered. They chit-chatted a bit, covering the basics of what had been happening with Billy, then Mike said, "So, Kristy, I called to tell you something."

"What's that?"

"I'm sorry."

"Sorry? For what?" She seemed surprised that the words came out of Mike's mouth. She hadn't heard them that often.

"I've been learning a few things here—and from the unlikeliest places—about some areas of my life I haven't been very good at."

"Oh yeah?"

"Yes. You know I've become friends with the football coach here."

"The *football coach?*"

"Yeah, it sounds funny, I'm sure, but he's really successful and we've been talking about leadership. He challenged me to think about how good of a leader I am at work, and . . . well, at home. One thing he said was that you get what you model, and I've realized that I haven't been the best model for you or for Billy and that has caused problems for us. It has also caused problems for me at work as well."

There was a long pause. Finally, Mike said, "So, do you have any response?"

"I was just thinking. It's surprising to hear you talking like this. You haven't really ever been very . . . self-aware."

"I know that. I'm sorry about that. Kristy, I want to be a good leader. I want work to go well here so I can get back up to Chicago. But more than anything, I want it to work out between us and we can have a great family with the three of us. I know a lot of that depends on me. I haven't been very good at it up till now, but I wanted to tell you that I'm learning and that I am sorry for what has happened in the past."

Kristy softened a little. "Okay, I forgive you . . . I'm not getting my hopes up too high, but you sound sincere enough. That seems like a good start."

"Well, thanks."

"You know," Kristy continued, "I have been thinking about a few things, too. I'd like to give it some more thought and then run it by you. Some things I could change myself."

"That sounds good. I'd like that . . . One more thing, Kristy."

"What's that?"

"How about you fly down for a long weekend, see one of Billy's games, hang out with us?"

"Let me think about it. I *would* like to see Billy. I miss him a lot."

"He misses you, too. Just come down. It'll be fun."

"All right, I will check on flights and see what would be a good weekend. You check the schedule and let me know what home games are coming up."

Mike was excited. "Okay, I will. I'll e-mail them to you!"

They talked a few more minutes and then agreed on another call in a few days. Mike thought it went well, and felt more excited than he had in weeks. After he hung up, he called Tanya and told her the good news—that Kristy had responded well to his overture.

CHAPTER 12

A few weeks into the season, East Creek was—as expected—4–0. Their first four games were won with ease against opponents that were quite overmatched. The next couple of weeks promised a bigger challenge. Mike decided to stop by the end of practice Monday afternoon to watch a little and then take Billy home. The end of Monday practice was always a fun part of the week and many parents came by.

Coach Logan always used the last fifteen minutes of Monday practice to recognize the best performances from Friday night's game, and players, coaches, and parents all looked forward to it. As everyone settled down on the bleachers, Coach Logan took a clipboard out of his bag and began to go through a list of awards he was giving.

He started out with the helmet stickers—football-shaped stickers, star stickers, and skull and crossbones stickers, all signifying great plays, big hits, and superb performances. Then Coach moved on to a number of small acrylic plaques, laser engraved with the player's name. And then the big awards, the game balls. Three of them: Offensive Player of the Game, Defensive Player of the Game, and Most Inspirational. Some people had wondered why not a Most Valuable Player, but Coach Logan always thought Most Inspirational was more important. And the kids loved to get it. Sometimes it was the star of the game. Sometimes it was a player who hadn't even gotten in the game but showed tremendous spirit and support. And sometimes it was even one of the younger ball boys or water boys. They were all a team and Coach Logan made sure they got rewarded for a job well done.

When the session was over, Mike asked Coach Logan if he had a few minutes.

"Sure, Mike, what's up?"

Mike turned to Billy. "I'll talk to Coach while you go get changed. Meet you at the car in a little bit." Billy jogged off to hit the showers.

"So, what's up, Mike?"

"Oh, nothing big, but I wanted to talk to you about this Monday afternoon ritual you have."

"Yeah, what about it?"

"I think it's a great idea. I think some people might think it was over the top, though. I mean, rewarding them with big awards every week."

"You're right, Mike, some people do think that, but then again, these are the same folks who go three and seven or two and eight every year. The proof's in the puddin'."

"No, no, I get it. I like it. And it's obvious the kids like it, too. Here's what I am wondering: Do you think it would work if I implemented something like this at MMC? I mean, would it work with adults?"

"Sure it would, Mike. This is a people thing. You know what I say, 'People's people.' There are simple things that go across the lines of the differences in people. I'll tell ya another leadership rule I follow: *You get what you reward*."

"Yeah, but . . ."

"Yeahbut? Is that like a rabbit? Think about *people*, Mike. If they think they're gonna get something out of it, they're gonna do it. You can get all fancy and try to come up with all sorts of different ways to explain the way people work, but what it comes down to is that people do what they get rewarded for."

"So, you're saying that those kids wouldn't play hard if you didn't give out the stickers and the game balls and such every Monday?"

"Not sayin' that, Mike. But what I *am* sayin' is that whether it's conscious or subconscious, they work *harder* because we give those rewards out. It is human nature to seek reward and recognition. People have a deep need to be seen for accomplishing something. It starts when you're potty trainin' a kid, then when they're in grade school, what does every kid look for on their homework? A star sticker. Kids are lookin' for reward and recognition. That doesn't end when you get out of high school. Grownups just cover it up better and pretend they don't need anything. They do, though. It's your job as the leader to find out what reward would motivate them."

"How do you find that out? Shouldn't it just be their paycheck? I mean, I'm paying them to do their jobs. That should be enough."

"Sure it should, if you lived in a perfect world. But you don't. Let's say you got a scale of one to a hundred, and one hundred equals perfect work every day. In a perfect world every single employee would come in every day and give a one hundred level performance because they get paid a paycheck. But they don't. Heck, Mike, I'll bet *you* don't, do you?"

"No, of course not."

"Well, there you go. So what would you say the average number would be that would describe the level of your employees on an average day?"

"Maybe seventy-five. They're pretty good."

"Seventy-five. That's average. That's a 'C' for a grade."

"I suppose that's about right. Some are better than others."

"All right, so that's the starting point. Your seventy-five average means you work at a certain level and make a certain amount of money for MMC. Now, the big question, what would happen if a year from now, you moved that average up to eighty or eighty-five? That means everybody is givin' another five or ten every single day. How would that change your plant? How would that increase the money you're makin' over there?"

Mike didn't say anything at first. He just stood there thinking about the possibilities. What *would* happen if he could get another 10 percent out of his people?

Coach continued, "I'm guessin' it would make you some more money and get you back to Chicago."

"Okay, agreed. So what do I do, Coach?"

Coach bent down and picked up a football. He started turning toward the locker room. "Mike, I can't do it all for you. That part you have to figure out for yourself. Get your team together at the plant, tell 'em you're gonna start a rewards program—call it what you want—and see what they think would work. Then tinker with it when you get it up and running to make it work better. Just be sure you follow through. They'll be skeptical at first since it's never been done before, but stick with it and it'll work." He was now twenty feet away from Mike. "Gotta go, Mike. Keep me posted."

When Mike and Billy got home, Mike decided to try something. During dinner he made Billy an offer. "Hey, Billy, I've been thinking."

"Yeah, Dad?"

"Yeah. Here's deal. We'll try it for one week. You know I don't like it when you play video games before you do your homework." It was a constant point of contention between them.

"Yeah . . ." Billy didn't know where this was going.

"For one week, if you do your homework *before* you play video games—that means football, then dinner, then homework, *then* video games—I will give you five dollars each day you do it. How's that sound?"

"You're kidding, right?"

"No, not at all."

"Dude, I am all over that. That's an easy thirty-five bucks a week."

"Did you just call me 'dude'?"

"Sorry, Dad. But yeah, I'll take that deal. Can I start tonight?"

Mike got a smile on his face. "Sure, you can start tonight."

Billy took his last few bites of dinner, got up and put his plate in the sink, and hustled off to make his "easy" $5.

"*You get what you reward,*" Mike said quietly. Now, how to get it to work at MMC?

The next morning Mike called his top five executives in and they came up with a plan to implement a rewards program for MMC. Mike called headquarters and asked them to sign off on the additional expenditure as a pilot program. A few days later they came back with an okay and Mike and his team scheduled an all-company meeting, bringing in all the shifts together for the first time in a long time. They rented the high school gym to hold the twelve hundred plus people.

Mike's idea was to make it a fun night. He arranged for pizza and soda to be brought in and hired a local country band with a good regional reputation to warm up the crowd. Then it came time for Mike to reveal the new plan for MMC's reward and recognition plan.

"Ladies and gentlemen, thanks for coming out tonight. I hope you got your fill of pizza!" The crowd cheered. "Now, I know this may be different, and I suppose it is, but we are going to be making some changes at MMC and I think you are going to like what we are doing. I have been very happy here the last few months as your leader. You are a great team to work with and our future is bright.

"I know that it can be tough to have an 'outsider' come in, but you have all been so very gracious to me. I had a few bumps at the beginning but we worked them out and we are on our way to a better and more profitable company.

"So, why call you all in here for this special night? Well, partly to thank you for what you've been doing, and partly to announce a new program that the leadership team, both here in East Creek and in Chicago, are very excited about. In fact, we here in East Creek are the pilot for this new program. Now, I know what some of you may be thinking: *Oh boy, another set of rules and regulations to follow*. Well, I have good news. That's not it at all. In fact, this new program is about you, the people who are the backbone of our company.

"I am proud to announce the brand-new MMC Reward and Recognition Program. This new program is based on the idea that people have a deep need to be recognized for the work, value, and contribution they bring to others. We have developed and secured funding from headquarters for a program that will recognize each and every person at MMC beyond just the paycheck they get. Now, you will all get a brochure explaining the whole program, but unfortunately, try as we might, we couldn't get them back from the printer in time for the meeting tonight. But let me give you the overview, and then we have a special speaker.

"We will be budgeting in rewards at every level for good performance, extra effort, excellent customer service, and safety. These rewards range from little items like gift certificates and coffee cards that will be given out spur of the moment by supervisors to medium-sized rewards like sporting goods, camping equipment, and video games, and all the way up to big rewards such as thousand-dollar bonuses and airline tickets. And we will be giving an Employee of the Year award: an all-expenses-paid cruise for the winner's family." The crowd cheered wildly. They had never seen something like this at MMC.

"Now, if you don't think that is enough, I have invited a guest speaker to tell you about what I consider to be our best reward, which will be given out annually. I have become friends with this gentleman the last few months and have learned a lot from him in that short time. Ladies and gentlemen, let me introduce to you someone who needs no introduction, our very own legend, Coach Logan of the East Creek Cougars!" All the MMC employees, most of whom had grown up in East Creek and many of whom had played for Coach Logan, jumped to their feet and started singing the East Creek fight song. It was almost like a typical Friday night at Cougar Stadium.

When Coach Logan got to the microphone he quickly fired up the crowd even further. "All right, everybody, let's hear one for good old East Creek!" They cheered. "And how about one for the company that has been the biggest employer here for decades, MMC!" They cheered again. "And, I can't resist it because we have what looks to me like a who's who of East Creek alumni, so let's hear one for the East Creek Cougars!" Even those who hadn't attended East Creek cheered.

"Thanks for having me in to talk to you tonight. I will make it short and sweet. I've gotten to know Mike a little the past few months and he's a good man. I have a whole lot of relatives at MMC, and it has been a pillar of our town for decades. We all appreciate what they have done for us. Tonight, Mike asked me to come in and announce the big award, the one that will be given once a year to an MMC employee.

"As you know, I am a big believer in inspiration. In fact, every week during the season, I give away our biggest award, the Most Inspirational Player. From now on, MMC will be giving a yearly

91

award to the Most Inspirational Employee. This can be any employee. It isn't reserved for the suits in the front office. Ultimately it's about attitude. This award is given to the employee who not only demonstrates a positive and enthusiastic attitude but inspires others to do the same. Whether it is in football or in the workplace, we need people who will inspire us to be and do our best. That is what makes winners!

"So, what is the award? I'll let Mike show you." At that moment, driving in through a big roll-up door opening into the auxiliary gym, was Mike Keller in a brand-new car, window rolled down and waving to the crowd. Every single employee was standing up again, screaming and clapping.

Mike parked the car, got out, and went back up on the stage to speak to his employees again. He thanked Coach Logan and filled in the details of the award. "Yes, it's true, from now on we will be giving away a car to the most inspirational employee. This is a $20,000 value. We give you the keys and you drive away. It isn't a lease, and you don't have to give it back. It will go to the person we believe is the employee who inspires us the most every year. I am excited about our new plan and I hope you are too!" Again, the crowd of employees roared in appreciation.

After a few more words, Mike wrapped up the meeting. There was a buzz in the crowd that there hadn't ever been. Mike knew they were on to something good.

CHAPTER 13

he next two months were a blur. MMC was experiencing some positive changes due to Mike's implementation of Coach's leadership rules. MMC employees began to respond positively over time as they stopped seeing Mike as simply an outsider. The level of work was already rising and the rewards program for work well done was all anyone could talk about. There was a brand-new mood and the outlook was good.

Mike was also making ground with Kristy. His phone call asking for forgiveness proved to be a turning point. They were now talking regularly, feeling a warmth they hadn't had in years. That made them all happy, but especially Billy.

And of course, the East Creek Cougars had continued their dominance of Texas State high school football. They were still undefeated four days out from their final regular season game. Practices this week would be intense and focused.

The team was continuing to get better each and every week; it was peaking at the right time.

Kristy flew down to East Creek to go to the game. She came in on Thursday for a three-day weekend with Mike and Billy. She was a little concerned about how she and Mike would get along but was very excited to see Billy. They had arranged for her to stay in the extra bedroom but they would eat together and stay together in order to put some work into the family relationship.

Of course, the highlight was the Friday night game. Billy wasn't starting but was getting some good game time on special teams and on relief for the starting weak safety. Cougar Stadium was abuzz with excitement as always on Friday nights. Mike and Kristy were in the stands on the forty-yard line—a great view of the game.

Kristy was overwhelmed. Until you have been to a big-time Texas high school football game, you can't imagine what it is like. Seeing is believing.

Luckily for Mike and Kristy, Billy started off with a bang. He was on the kickoff coverage team; once the ball was in the air, Billy started weaving down the field looking for the angle on the return. At about the twenty-two-yard line, the young man with the football stopped and made a quick turn back in the other direction. Unfortunately for him, it was at the same time Billy came through the last blocker and ball carrier met Billy with a very loud sound of helmets and pads. The other player went backwards with force and the ball went flying into the air. The crowd went wild and the scramble was on for the loose ball. The Cougars didn't recover, though, and the starting defense went onto the field. Kristy was going crazy for her boy, and as he trotted off his teammates gave him the congratulatory smack on the pads. Billy, however, looked to the stands to see that his folks had seen it. It was clear that they had, and the best was yet to come.

Shortly into the fourth quarter, Billy came in to give the starting weak safety some rest. On his second play in the lineup, the opposing team's quarterback dropped back to pass, looked to his primary receiver—and then back to his secondary receiver when the primary was covered. Billy was playing loose and the quarterback set to throw to a player in front of Billy. As he was setting to throw, he got more pressure from the defensive line, forcing him back a little just as he threw, which took some of the zip off the throw. That gave Billy just the time he needed, and he played it perfectly—cutting in front of the receiver and intercepting the pass. Because he was on the weak side, he had nothing but end zone in front of him. The opposition's only chance to catch him at that point would have been the quarterback, and that young man was firmly ensconced on his rear end, with a couple of very happy Cougar linemen on top of him, keeping him there.

Seconds later, Billy was alone in the end zone and the Cougars added six more points to their already big lead. In the grand scheme of the game, it wasn't the turning point, but it was about the best thing that could have happened the night his mom was in town.

After the game, Billy was going to go out with some friends, so Kristy and Billy decided to go to Joey's Malt Shop and meet Billy back at the house later.

Kristy and Mike settled into a booth after ordering their milk shakes. Banana for Kristy, chocolate for Mike. "That was some game," Kristy said.

"Boy, I know. That's big-time football for you here in Texas."

"I can't believe how big the stadium is. It's huge. My high school's football field sat maybe five hundred people. Just some bleachers on the side of the field."

Mike leaned in a little toward Kristy. "I'm so glad you came down this weekend, Kristy. We miss you very much."

Kristy looked away, not wanting to make eye contact. She missed Mike and Billy too, but didn't want to let on. There had been a growing distance in their marriage that left her hurt, and she didn't want to let Mike back in too quickly. Mike reached out and touched her hand. She turned back to look at him, her eyes a bit wet.

"Kristy, we really miss you."

"I miss you, too."

"Can I tell you what one of my goals is?"

"Sure."

"I want to win you back. Kristy, you mean everything to me. I know I haven't been what I could be or what you want me to be, but I want to change. I am working on changing. Believe it or not, getting sent down here has actually been pretty good for me."

"Oh?"

"Yeah, I have gotten to know the football coach, Coach Logan, and he has taught me a lot about leadership."

"You're *learning* leadership from the high school football coach?"

"The seventeen-time Texas State High School Champion football coach. *Big* difference."

"So what are you learning?"

"I'm learning that I get what I put into it. I get what I expect to get. I get what I model. I get what I reward."

"How has that helped you?"

"Well, I'll give you two examples. I know that I will get what I expect with you. I'd given up. I just expected we would get divorced. Now I expect that we are going to get together. That expectation changes everything. Now I work toward what I expect."

"And what is the other way it has helped you?"

"With work. I get what I reward. I implemented a new recognition and reward program that goes down through the whole company and people are really excited about it. The whole mood of the plant has changed. It hasn't been going long enough to know yet, but I expect—there's that word again—that it is going to do big things for our plant."

The waitress came to the table and dropped off the milk shakes. "Anything else I can get you folks?" she asked.

"Nope, that's good. Thanks," said Mike.

Kristy picked up the conversation. "Well, that's good that you are learning. I will tell you that we do have some things to work on, but if you are willing to work on them, I am too. And it sounds like this football coach is good for you."

"Yeah, he is. He's a good guy. Funny, you know, at first a guy like me comes down here, educated, from the city, corporate type, and you look down at a guy like Coach Logan. That was my first lesson. I realized I was a little snooty and thought I knew it all. Who knew?"

Kristy and Mike spent the next hour catching up on what was going on in Chicago, how Billy was doing in school, and the updates on all of the extended family and their goings-on. When they were done with their milk shakes, they went home to meet Billy, though he didn't get home for another hour after they did.

CHAPTER 14

Mike decided to go to work early during the final week so he could get over to the practices and help out. A number of other fathers did the same. The Cougars had won all of their playoff games and now had just one game left. The Championship. Monday's practice ended the same as it always did, with the rewards for the last game. Tuesday's practice started differently, though. Coach Logan called the team together to talk to them.

"Men, congratulations. You have accomplished something that ninety-nine percent of players your age never do: You made it to a State Championship football game. You're undefeated. But you're not done. In fact you're a long way from being done. We're only at base camp as far as I'm concerned. Over the course of the next four days, we are going to climb the highest mountain we have ever climbed together. I am going to push you harder than you have ever been pushed before. You think three-a-days were tough last summer? Not even close to what I will be asking from you this week.

"In the next week you will become great. You will become leaders. You will rise up to the highest level you can push yourselves to. You've heard me say it before, my leadership rule: *You get what you work for*. You've worked hard—but now you have to work harder. The other side is at practice right now. They have one goal: To beat us Saturday afternoon. Not just to beat us, but to destroy us. They want to conquer us. They want to humiliate us in defeat. They want this. We have to want it more. It begins and ends with your desire. You have to want it like you've never wanted anything. You have the skills. You know the play. You know how to execute. But what we will find out this week is how badly you want it. And how hard you are willing to work for it.

"Wanting it isn't enough. What separates the successful from the unsuccessful—the men from the boys, so to speak—is hard work. My question for you is simply, 'Will you work hard enough for it?' Each and every moment of practice this week I'm asking for your one hundred percent concentration. If the cheerleaders walk by, you keep your attention on me. I'm asking for your one hundred percent effort. One hundred percent discipline. Focus on the goal, men. Outwork your opponent. We have a plan. We have a strategy. Now it's time to execute. The coaching staff worked all weekend to get ready. We are prepared. The question is whether or not you young men will step up to the challenge ahead.

"In the end those who work the hardest are the ones who win. They don't win every time, but that's where I'll put my money every time. Ninety-six hours from now you will either be the Texas State Champion Football Team, or you will be second place. The three hours of the game count, but the days leading up to those three hours count too. So let's make the most of these practices, men. They make the difference between winners and losers. Now let's bring it in."

That was the sign that the talk was over and the hard work was to begin. All the young men gathered in a tight circle. They flopped their heavily padded arms over each other's shoulders, and bent over at the waist. A low murmur began. They rocked back and forth, left to right. It was mesmerizing to watch. Up and down, back and forth, louder and louder. Then it came to crescendo and the players shouted "Cougars! Champs!" and threw their hands in the air. They broke out of their huddle and ran en masse to the center of the field, where they began to go through their calisthenics.

Mike watched with interest as the team exercised and warmed up. He was excited. He had never experienced anything like this when he played sports. About the furthest any of his teams ever made it was the first round of the playoffs. And he had never experienced anything like it in work. He loved the feeling of success. Admittedly, he was living vicariously through Billy. And it was *fun*.

CHAPTER 15

It was halftime of the State Championship football game. The Cougars were deep inside Texas Stadium in a locker room normally reserved for the professional football teams that played there. It was overwhelming, to be sure. After a brutal first half filled with hard hits, blood, and injuries, the Cougars, who were the heavy favorites to win, were down 21–17. Coach Logan was not happy.

"Men, that was not the kind of first half I was lookin' for. We got outhit, outrun, outblocked, outhustled, out *everything*. This is exactly what we worked all week to make sure wouldn't happen. You worked hard all week. I'll give you that. But for the first half, it was like you weren't there. You are in this game partly because you are so talented. But that other team is talented too. And right now, their desire and hard work is allowing their talent to win the ball game for them." Coach Logan then spent some time talking specifics about what they had done right and wrong and how they could improve.

Just before they were to head back out onto the field, Coach Logan said, "Gentlemen, this is the last talk I'm going to give you. This is the last halftime of the season. Some of you will never play football again. This is *it*. I can't get out there and play for you. You have to outwork these kids across the line of scrimmage from you. Hit harder, block harder, run faster. You get what you work for. Now go out there and take your destiny into your hands. You have to choose whether you are going to lay it all on the line and leave yourselves completely spent on that field."

The team gathered together, did their chant, then hit the field.

CHAPTER 16

I t was Wednesday morning, four days after the East Creek Cougar football team gave Coach Logan his eighteenth Texas State Football Championship, 38–21. It had been a close game through the first half, but not long into the second it became obvious that Coach Logan's leadership rules had paid off.

The players came to play that second half. They knew that the Coach had high expectations of them. They had high expectations of themselves.

They executed on what they had seen their coaches live all year long. Coach Logan and the rest of the staff had modeled what it meant to be champions and now they were champions themselves.

The promise of the reward was palpable. Everything they had looked forward to had come down to that second half and they wouldn't be denied. Every practice, every game, every lesson learned found fruition in the prospect of being a champion.

They got what they'd worked for. All year long they'd put in hard work, starting with three practices a day under the hot August sun. The week before the Championship Game was just like Coach Logan said it would be: Hard work.

Mike was sitting in his office at MMC when his phone rang.

"Hello, this is Mike."

"Mike, good news." It was Mike's boss in Chicago.

"Yeah, what's that?"

"Corporate just got the latest numbers and they look good. We just got out of a meeting and everyone agreed that if you keep it up six more months, we'll move you back to Chicago."

"Really? That's fantastic!"

"Now, it's not a guarantee, but it is in the works. You just keep the ship going in the right direction and you'll get back to Chicago."

"Wow. That would be great."

"One more thing. Keep it to yourself for now. We are thinking of moving Tyler up when we bring you back. So work on giving him more responsibility and bring him even more into decision making. We'd like to make his promotion seamless when we bring you back."

"Sure, I'll do that. No problem. Thanks so much for the call."

"You bet, Mike. You've done a good job and you rose to the occasion. To be honest, I didn't know how you'd respond to being sent down there."

"Well, I've learned a lot down here from the unlikeliest places. I'll tell you all about it when I get back."

"Sounds like a deal, Mike." They hung up and Mike floated through the day, looking forward to his phone call with Kristy that night.

CHAPTER 17

K risty, great news!"

"Oh, do tell."

"I think it's great, anyway. Billy and I are probably coming back to Chicago in six months." He didn't know how she would respond. They had been getting along better and the distance seemed to do them some good. The old saying, "Distance makes the heart grow fonder," seemed to be true. Of course, Mike had been working hard at restoring the relationship with lots of phone conversation. He especially tried to follow Tanya's suggestion and listen more.

He continued. "Now, you don't need to make a decision right now, but I'm hoping you'll consider something."

"Sure, what?"

"Would you consider letting Billy and me move back in with you? It would give us a chance to make it work. We've made up a lot of ground long distance these last few months, right?"

"Yes, I think we have." She passed for a few seconds before continuing, "I'll think about it. That would probably be a good thing."

Mike pumped his fist, and Tanya—who had walked in through the back door while he was on the phone—pressed her hands to her mouth to suppress a squeal of excitement. Mike and Kristy talked a few more minutes before hanging up and agreeing to talk more later in the week about the potential of getting back together.

As soon as he hung up, Tanya shrieked. "She said yes, didn't she? I knew she would say yes. I'm a good coach, ain't I?"

"Well, hold on. She didn't say yes, but she did open the door to it happening."

"That means yes. She isn't just going to out-and-out let you back so easy. She'll play hard to get, but you'll get her back. And we have six more months to work on you so you can get her back for good."

"Boy, Tanya, Kristy doesn't know what a good friend she has in you. Someday I hope you meet her. It's too bad you were out of town the weekend she came down. You've been a good coach. You've helped me understand some things I didn't know before."

"Oh yeah, Dr. Phil ain't got nothin' on me."

CHAPTER 18

F riday morning Mike walked into the plant and got a big surprise. In fact, a surprise party—for him. The people at the plant were warming up to him and the changes he was making, and so, in the spirit of the reward and recognition program, they'd decided to give him some recognition. They had cake and coffee, and a few folks got up and said good things about him and his leadership. It actually made Mike tear up. He had never had anything like that happen before.

One of the line leaders got up and talked. Mike didn't really know more than her name, Michelle Yates. "Mr. Keller, I just want to say that I am really glad that you are our boss now. It used to be that I dreaded coming to work. It wasn't a lot of fun and I felt like I was stuck. All I could do is make my hourly wage. But you have made it fun. And now you have made it so I can make more money and be rewarded for my efforts. I'm a single mom and I need everything I can get. I don't want to work nights and leave my kids at home. MMC is a great place to work. Thanks for being a great leader and making these changes."

Mike couldn't believe it. These people liked him. And he liked them too.

After the party, as everyone was getting back to work, Tyler asked Mike if he could talk to him in private. After the door closed, Tyler said, "Can I talk to you about something?"

"Sure, Tyler. What's up?"

"Well, it looks like I'm going to be moving down to Dallas."

"Dallas, what for?"

"I got an offer to go work for my father-in-law in the family business. It's twice the money—and he's getting older and wants a family member to take it over. My wife's brother doesn't want it, so they offered it to me."

"So it looks like you are moving or you *are* moving."

"I am moving."

"When?"

"A couple months."

"Okay. We sure are going to miss you. Have you told corporate?"

"No, not yet. I wanted to talk to you first."

"Okay, be sure to call them and let them know."

Mike didn't know how that was going to fit corporate's plan for the plant when he moved back up to Chicago. But that was their problem.

His cell phone rang, and he hit the no-hands switch. "Hello, this is Mike."

"Mike, Coach Logan."

"Oh, hey, Coach, what's up? Still basking in the glory of the victory?"

"Nope, already planning for next year. I give myself a day to enjoy it. Then it's back to business. That's why I'm calling."

"Oh yeah, whaddaya need?"

"Can you swing by my office?"

"Sure. Billy's out with friends tonight and I was just headed home. I'll swing by in five minutes."

"Great, I'll talk to you then."

"So what do you want to talk about, Coach?"

"Mike, I'll cut straight to it. I have a couple coaches retiring and I'm gonna be a bit short-handed. I could use you next year to help coach."

"You mean more than watch video?"

"Yes sir. I mean being a full-fledged coach. I figure since you are the boss at MMC you can arrange to get off early for the season. Go in early so you put in the day and then come coach. It's a big commitment, but I wanted to ask you to do it. What do you think?"

"Wow, well it's very humbling. That you would even ask me is great. I would love to but . . ."

"But what?"

"Well, Coach, I don't know that I'll be here next year."

"Won't be here? What are you talking about? You're not going back to Chicago, are you?"

"Well, as a matter of fact . . ."

"Oh come on, Mike, you're just getting started. MMC needs you and your leadership. You can't leave now. Besides, East Creek is starting to like you."

"What do you mean *starting* to like me?"

"Well, this is a small town. People talk. It's hard moving here from out of town. Hard to break in, you know? People didn't like you much when you got here. But three months into it, what with all the changes you are making and all, people are starting to like you. Billy's settling in well here, and the kids really like him, too."

"That's great and all, but you know, I'm a Chicago boy. I really want to get back there, back with my wife."

"You know what I think?"

"No, what?"

"I think you should stay here at least another year."

"Why?"

"A couple of reasons. One, Billy will be a senior next year; it's hard on a kid to be moving back and forth, especially senior year. Second, the people at MMC will think you are abandoning them. They have committed themselves to you now, and they would feel used."

"I can appreciate that. I don't know, though."

"And here's another one for you."

"Yeah, what's that?"

"I think you ought to ask your wife to move down here with you."

"Okay, Coach, now you're off your rocker. That will never happen."

"Really, you get what you expect. Remember that."

"Well, I *expect* Kristy will tell me I'm crazy if I suggest it to her."

"I got a steak dinner says she'll do it."

"Coach, you're nuts—with all due respect. She won't do it. Kristy is the ultimate city girl."

"That's just because she's never lived in a small town."

"I'll give you that small town living far exceeded my expectations, but Kristy? Never happen."

"Never hurts to ask."

"Coach, why are you pushing me to do this?"

"I'll tell you why. I'm a good judge of people. No, I'm a *great* judge of people. I see what you are trying to accomplish, what you are trying to be, and it won't ever make you happy, Mike. You're a small town guy who grew up in the city. You just didn't know you were a small town guy. Now you do. It will be good for you, Billy, Kristy, your family. And you can quit doing 'fantasy football' and live your fantasy with real-life big-time Texas high school football."

That struck a chord. Mike knew there was truth to what Coach was saying. He'd had this idea of what he had wanted to do with his career, but he had never been fulfilled in pursuing it. And he hadn't been very successful in fulfilling it, either.

"Okay, Coach, because I respect you and I do think you are a good judge of people, I'll ask her. And I'll take that steak dinner bet that she tells me absolutely no."

"Sounds like a deal. You call her and let me know."

Mike got up and started out the door. Just as he grabbed the doorknob, Coach said, "Oh, and Mike . . ."

Mike turned. "Yeah?"

"I like Smokey's."

"Huh?"

"Smokey's Steak House. They have a Tuesday night special. That will save you some money on the dinner you're gonna owe me."

Mike laughed and left without another word.

CHAPTER 19

The night after Coach asked Mike to ask Kristy to move down to East Creek, Mike was just about wrapping up a phone call with her when he decided to bring it up. He had to admit that they had been getting along and that reconciliation was certainly what he expected would happen. "Hey Kristy?"

"Yeah?"

"One last thing. And I know you're gonna think it's crazy, but I want to run something by you."

"Okay . . ."

"Look, I really like it down here. The people are great and MMC is going great. It seems like you and I are getting back on track . . ."

"And . . . just say it."

"I'm wondering what you would think about moving down here to East Creek so we could start over down here."

Silence.

"Kristy?"

"I'm here. I'm just thinking."

"What are you thinking? You're thinking I'm crazy, right?"

"No, not at all. My boss called me in the other day and said he was going to need to lay me off because business is so bad. He gave me a month's notice and two months' severance."

"Really? Wow, I'm sorry to hear that."

"And, well, I kind of liked East Creek. I've never lived in a small town before. It was neat."

"Are you saying you would consider it? Really?"

"Yeah, I'd consider it. What the heck? Life is short."

"Unbelievable. Really? You would really move down here?"

"It's crazy, but if we're going to start over, let's really start over."

"You're serious? Really? Wow."

"I'll finish up here with work, sell the house, and away we go."

"Unbelievable. That's fantastic!"

They decided to make plans later in the week and figure out how to tell Billy.

Mike picked up the phone and called Coach Logan. When Coach answered, Mike said, "So, how do you like your steak?"

Coach didn't miss a beat. "Medium rare."

"Well, make the reservations. She said she'd move here."

"I knew she would. That's great, Mike. Or, as I'll call you from now on, Coach Mike."

"Coach Mike. I like that."

"Glad to have you on board, Coach Mike. You can help me get number nineteen."

"Number nineteen, here we come!"

PART TWO

THE LESSONS

SECOND HALF

One of the concepts I believe in strongly is the transferability of principles across the segments of life. As I write books and speak at events around the United States and the world, I always focus in on the three primary areas that affect us most. As we look at general success principles and specifically the leadership rules, we find that they work in these three areas. It isn't that you do one thing at work and another thing at home. The principles work across the board:

- In the business we are in
- In the family we belong to
- In the social groups we are involved in

Whether you are applying the leadership rules to your business, your parenting, or your PTA, you'll find they transcend the different areas of life and work across the board.

As Coach Logan would say, "People's people." Yes, we are all different, but we also have similarities that govern behavior.

What follows are some of my personal thoughts on the leadership rules and how you can apply them in your own leadership situations. What I tell my audiences is that not every single point is going to strike a chord with you, and that's okay. Not each one will be pertinent to you. All will be helpful, but some will stand out to you. When you read them, your heart will speak to you and you will hear yourself say, "That's one I need to learn and apply." When that thought hits you, slow down. Take your time reading. Spend some time thinking about how that particular principle will help you change your leadership and take it to the next level.

LEADERSHIP RULE NUMBER ONE

YOU GET WHAT YOU EXPECT

Getting what you expect may seem intuitively obvious—but people rarely act as though they believe it. The rule has several implications for daily life:

- Set and follow your own expectations.
- Set expectations and hold others to them.
- Remember that expectations create ownership.
- Be straightforward and honest.
- Set expectations that lead people to their own greatness.

- Make expectations big enough to motivate, small enough to achieve.
- Consider the strengths and weaknesses of your team.
- Be a visionary who can cast a vision.

FOLLOWING THE RULE

Set and follow your own expectations. As the leader, you need to know for yourself what your expectations are. Do you know? Are you clear with them yourself? If not, that is the place to start. Do you have expectations for yourself? Do you live up to your own expectations? If not, that is job one. Then you can move to leading others.

Set expectations and hold others to them. One of my favorite stories of a leader setting expectations and sticking to them, even when it concerned one of the best basketball players in history, is the story of John Wooden (legendary coach of UCLA) and player Bill Walton, and Walton's desire to have a beard in spite of team rules against it. As the story goes, Walton showed up at practice with a beard, clearly in violation of the expectations set forth for the team. When Wooden confronted

132

him on it, Walton declared that it was his right. Wooden responded by saying, "Bill, I respect people who stand up for what they believe, and the team is going to miss you." Then he went back to coaching the rest of the team. Guess who went and shaved his beard?

When we set expectations, there will always be those who push the boundaries to see if they can get away with their own rules. It's especially hard when a star performer is the one to push the limits. Don't give in. The rest of the team is watching the leader. If you hold your ground, they will respect you, and most likely, so will the person who was pushing back on your expectations.

Remember that expectations create ownership. Leaders who are successful create a sense of ownership among the people who follow them. This can be done in a lot of ways. First, while it is the leader's prerogative to set the expectations, it is always helpful to incorporate the thoughts of the people who follow into the expectations that are set for the group. This creates buy-in and gets people on board with the direction you are taking. It also gets people on board with policing the expectations by creating a culture that people expect each other to fit into. When clarifying your expectations, have individual and group meetings with key people, leading them through the process of coming to expectations for the group. Then it isn't just you laying down the law, it is a process that all are involved with and creates ownership through the ranks.

Be straightforward and honest. The only thing worse than a leader with no expectations is a leader who has expectations but isn't clear, straightforward, and honest about them. I know all the reasons why people struggle with this as leaders, but none are good reasons. Leadership requires courage and the forthrightness to look people in the eye and be straight with them. If you haven't made your expectations clear, you can't expect people to follow them. Not only do you owe it to your people, both you and they will be better served if you do.

Set expectations that lead people to their own greatness. Low expectations are a dime a dozen. There is a reason why most of the world exists in average, mediocrity, and status quo: people mostly have low expectations of themselves and others. Organizations that excel are organizations that set high expectations. I know some leaders worry that if they ask a lot, their people won't follow. The reverse is actually true. People are looking to achieve greatness. They want to be challenged. They want to live for something greater than themselves. Mediocrity is a long, slow death. Leaders who challenge people to strive for greatness get one of two responses, both of which are okay. Some people really don't want to grow, and they leave—or drag their feet until forced to do so. That's okay, you don't want them on your team anyway. They'll just be a drain on the vision. Others do want to follow. They want to grow and stretch. They want to be a part of something big. Lead toward greatness and many will follow. Big expectations create committed followers.

Make expectations big enough to motivate, small enough to achieve. The question arises, "How big should an expectation be?" There is a danger at both ends of the spectrum. On one end you set an expectation that is so small that people reach it more or less by accident; no one really follows it. It doesn't inspire. On the other end you set an expectation that is so big it can't be met. It ends up discouraging people as they fail. So here is the key: Set your expectations big enough to motivate people but small enough that they can actually live up to them. It will take some work by you, the leader, but it is well worth the thoughtfulness. You can also make adjustments as you go along. You can raise or lower the bar to find the sweet spot that gets the most out of your followers.

Consider the strengths and weaknesses of your team. Certainly one of the things the leader must do is be realistic when setting expectations. This doesn't mean the leader isn't optimistic. That is a common misperception, that optimism and realism are mutually exclusive. They aren't. We can be optimistic about where we can go, but we must also be realistic as to where we are. One of the tasks of the leader is to make a good and honest assessment of the strengths and weaknesses of those who follow. Our expectations should play to the strengths of our followers so they can achieve and live up to those expectations. It doesn't mean that we make them small expectations, but that the strengths of the people will allow them to stretch and reach those expectations.

Be a visionary who can cast a vision. People toss the word *vision* around a lot when talking about leadership, and rightly so. A leader has to be able to set and cast a vision. You have two areas to focus on here: your character and your skills. That is, who you are and what you do. Being a great leader as it relates to vision is based on those two areas. First, be a visionary. Do you have big dreams? Do you think in terms of big accomplishments? Do you have high hopes? Those come from the core of who you are. Second, you need to be able to *cast* that vision: to learn and develop the skills required to be able to articulate the vision you have framed. What good is a vision in the leader's heart if it never gets across to people who follow? Not much good at all.

So, get your vision. Think big. Set your expectations for achieving that vision—for yourself and then for others. Then learn to communicate the vision and expectations to others. Work on your speaking. Work on your writing. Work on all of your communication skills so you can get your message across to others so that they understand it and are inspired by it.

MY FAVORITE QUOTES
ABOUT EXPECTATIONS

Whatever we expect with confidence becomes
our own self-fulfilling prophecy.
—BRIAN TRACY

The amazing thing about expectations is the self-fulfilling nature of them. Now, granted, this isn't a 100 percent guarantee, but I have found it to be true that if you expect to lose, you will lose, and if you expect to win, you will win. I don't know exactly how it works, but my best analysis is that the expectation, rooted in your mind, works at a subconscious level to make it come to pass. If you expect to win, your attitude and actions will reflect that expectation and will move you closer to winning.

Don't bunt. Aim out of the ball park. Aim for
the company of immortals.
—DAVID OGILVY

I love this insight from a famed advertising mogul, David Ogilvy. He, like many other success-ful people, knows that if you want to win big, you have to aim big. Little expectations produce little results, while big expectations produce big results. If you tell your team that you expect them to finish last, they will prove you right. However, if you tell them that you expect them to be champions, they will aim to become champions!

> Treat a man as he is, he will remain so. Treat a man the way he can be and ought to be, and he will become as he can be and should be.
> —JOHANN WOLFGANG VON GOETHE

There is something to the idea that people rise to the level at which you believe in them. I was very fortunate in my early years right out of college to have some very successful people believe in me. It was truly life changing. To have people of such high caliber treat me not as I was but as what I could be gave me the belief in myself to become the person they saw in me. When we as leaders place expectations on people it is because we believe that they can become something greater. We believe that they can perform and live at a higher level. That is a privilege of leadership, that we get to believe in people even before they believe in themselves.

Today, and every day, deliver more than you are
getting paid to do. The victory of success will be
half won when you learn the secret of putting
out more than is expected in all that you do.

—OG MANDINO

The only thing better than meeting expectations is *exceeding* expectations! Mandino, one
of the great success writers of all time, reminds
us that the bulk of success comes from doing
more than what is expected. That is true both for
us and for our followers. If you are expected to
sell a thousand units, sell two thousand. If you are
expected to give a good presentation, give a great
presentation! If you are expected to put in an hour,
put in two hours. Exceeding expectations is the
quick route to success.

We must learn to reawaken and keep ourselves
awake, not by mechanical aid, but by an infinite
expectation of the dawn.

—HENRY DAVID THOREAU

I love that wording: *Infinite expectation of
the dawn!* When does dawn come? Right after the
darkness! When things look dark, we can't give

in to pessimism and the thought that the hardship will continue. No, instead we know—and expect—that the darkness won't continue forever, and that the dawn is on its way! And that positive, optimistic expectation, of ourselves and others, is what reawakens our vision for what we can do and what we can become!

> If we did the things we are capable of, we
> would astound ourselves.
> —THOMAS EDISON

Most people expect that their lives will be average. Edison knew that human potential is virtually endless. I think maybe even Edison would be shocked by how far we have come from his early inventions. He did, however, know that we are capable of far greater things than what we are currently doing. Where we are now is only the platform for where we will be, both as individuals and as societies. We must simply expect more from ourselves. While I wasn't alive when it happened, one of the greatest moments in human history was when President Kennedy said that we would put a man on the moon. A man on the moon? Come on! Yet, we were capable of doing it, and we did. We expected it. We did it.

Questions for Reflection

- Are you clear about the expectations that you have for yourself, including both your work and your family?
- Have you made your expectations clear to those you lead?
- In what ways are you holding your followers accountable for the expectations you have for them?

LEADERSHIP RULE NUMBER TWO

YOU GET WHAT YOU MODEL

Expectations are all very well, but it doesn't matter what you think you expect from other people if you aren't visibly expecting it from yourself as well. People will use you as a model, so you need to follow several principles:

- Live yourself what you expect others to live.
- Set standards of excellence for yourself.
- Remember that you can only lead people to where you are, not beyond.
- Teach people as you model.

FOLLOWING THE RULE

Live yourself what you expect others to live. Being seen as a hypocrite has destroyed many a leader. In fact, it has taken out many great leaders. People who say one thing and do another, or who have a set of expectations for their followers that they themselves do not follow, are not looked upon highly. Leaders who want to gain and keep the trust of their followers must live what they speak of. Here's the rub: None of us are perfect. All of us have failed. All of us have said and done things that we wish we hadn't. All leaders make mistakes, even the great ones. So what is the balance? We should all set high expectations for ourselves and for others. We should all strive to live by those the best we can. And yet, sometimes we don't. What do we make of that? Do everything you can to follow your own advice. And when you fail, admit it. People know that their leaders are human and will make mistakes. They can live with that as long as the leader gets it. But if leaders think they don't have to live by their own words, that's when people abandon ship. Remember, what you model is what others see and follow.

Set standards of excellence for yourself. Excellence is attractive. People are drawn to people who embody excellence. Do you remember the old television show, *Lifestyles of the Rich and Famous?* Why did so many people tune in every week? Because people are attracted to the best things in life. They like nice clothes, cars, boats, and homes. People want more for themselves and are attracted to people who have achieved much. So when you are a leader, your job is to first set standards of excellence for yourself—and live them—so when other people see your life and work and say to themselves, "That's what I want," what they do helps your business achieve its goals. Think about when you want to grow in a particular area of your life. You seek out someone who has already excelled in that area and ask how you can get there too. That's what we can do as leaders. Live it so others want it. Then they follow.

Remember that you can only lead people to where you are, not beyond. The job of the leader is to be out front. The leader has to be ahead of the group so as to point the way. John Maxwell, one of the great writers on leadership, puts it this way: If you are a seven, you can only lead people to be sevens. You can't lead them to become eights. So the job is to make ourselves into eights and nines and tens so that we can raise the standard for others and bring them to what we have ourselves already attained.

Teach people as you model. You have probably heard the term "teachable moments." As leaders we set the vision for others and bring them along with us. This isn't a one-time thing, though. Along the way there will be countless opportunities to teach people about how to change and how to achieve the goals you have set for the organization. Leaders first live it, then they teach it. And they don't teach it just once and hope that people get it. They teach it over and over and over again as they progress through the journey. The job of teaching is rarely over.

MY FAVORITE QUOTES ON BEING AN EXAMPLE

Setting an example is not the main means of influencing another, it is the only means.

—ALBERT EINSTEIN

Is there a better example of this than being a parent? As the father of four children, setting a constant example is the scariest thing I face. I know that what I do speaks far louder than what I say. So I say what I believe and try my best to instill values in my children, but I also must do my best to live what I say. Like everyone, I have made my share of mistakes. When we as leaders make those mistakes we must make sure that we address them and correct them so our followers do not begin to see us as hypocrites. Followers do not expect us to be perfect, but they do expect us to live by what we say and admit it when we don't. People see what we do and follow that.

> A good example is the best sermon.
> —BENJAMIN FRANKLIN

Which is more effective: Telling people to feed the poor or feeding the poor? Telling people to forgive others or actually extending forgiveness to one who has wronged you? Yes, we should promote values such as compassion and forgiveness, but the best way to promote

147

those things—and any other values we desire to promote—is to set the example ourselves. Mother Teresa said, "In all things witness of Christ, and if necessary, use words." While she was speaking of religion, the same is true of the workplace. *In all things witness of hard work, and if necessary, use words.* In other words, set the example by working hard yourself.

> He that gives good advice, builds with one hand; he that gives good counsel and example, builds with both.
> —FRANCIS BACON SR.

Yes, people will learn from you if you teach them. Words are powerful things and can move people in tremendous ways. But you can increase your influence exponentially by adding good example to your good counsel. Unfortunately, as is true with all too many leaders, Bacon didn't take the advice himself— and his career ended in disgrace. We should all set out to build a long-term ability to lead by combining words and actions into a powerful force for influence.

Questions for Reflection

- Do you consider yourself a good example or not? Why?
- In what ways can you become a better example to others?
- How closely are you taking your own advice? Are you living what you expect from others?

LEADERSHIP RULE NUMBER THREE
YOU GET WHAT YOU REWARD

To get more of what you expect and model, it is useful to provide some extrinsic motivation to give the desired conduct a try. To key into the motivational benefits of reward, follow these principles:

- Understand the power of reward.
- Make the rewards known in advance.
- Tailor rewards to each recipient's interests if possible.
- Follow through on promised rewards.
- Make the rewards public.

FOLLOWING THE RULE

Understand the power of reward. Almost from birth, we respond to rewards for behavior. That's the way people work. Now, am I suggesting that people shouldn't work for altruistic reasons? No, certainly not. But I am saying that rewards are a part of life. Whether it is a kind word, money, public acknowledgment or recognition, or another type of reward, people respond to receiving a reward for what they have done. Yes, they also like the satisfaction of a job well done, but they can have that and a reward from the leader as well. Grownups are just that: grown-up children. A star on the paper doesn't work anymore, but a more creative reward will go a long way.

Make the rewards known in advance. A reward announced and given afterward will be appreciated, but a reward announced beforehand will be *worked for*. Be sure that all the rewards that your employees have available to them are well known before the effort that earns them. This will cement the pursuit in their minds and act as not only a conscious carrot but as a subconscious one as well. When they think of the work or task they need to perform, they will immediately connect it with the potential reward of accomplishing the work. This will make them more likely to do it.

Tailor rewards to each recipient's interests if possible. I remember working with a sales group a number of years ago out east. They had one sales guy who hadn't hit his quarterly numbers in years. They had offered him all sorts of bonuses but nothing ever seemed to motivate the guy. I asked what kinds of things he was personally interested in, and it turned out that he and his wife liked to travel. So I suggested to the owner that he offer the man a cruise if he hit his numbers the next quarter. The cost of the cruise was actually less than the amount of the bonuses he'd been offered. Guess who hit his numbers the next quarter? Yep, he did. The idea is to make rewards connect with people. Yes, they all like money, but sometimes people can be motivated more effectively by other things. Give those ideas a try and see if you get more from your followers.

Follow through on promised rewards. If you promise, you must deliver, so make sure that when people perform the work, they get the reward. It would be a big mistake to promise something and then not deliver 100 percent. Make sure that when you announce the reward that you have the resources available to make the reward actually happen.

Make the rewards public. Private reward and recognition will be appreciated, but public reward and recognition will be remembered for a very long time. I always suggest having a specific time each week or each month that people know is going to be when the members of the group are rewarded for their achievements. For many, this will be the only time they get public recognition for their contribution. Reward and recognition are like water over dry ground. They just sink right in and refresh. One of the great opportunities we have as leaders is to hold people up and see that they get the enjoyment of public recognition and appreciation.

MY FAVORITE QUOTES ON THE POWER OF REWARD

There are two things people want more than sex and money: recognition and praise.
—MARY KAY ASH

154

You probably remember Maslow's hierarchy of needs. Near the very top is the respect of others, confidence, and self-esteem. Mary Kay Ash, founder of the hugely successful Mary Kay line of cosmetics, clearly knew this. Yes, there are basic needs, but at a deeper level, people gain real satisfaction from knowing that they have accomplished something and made a contribution, and that they are recognized by their peers for that contribution. As you build your organization, understand that people are looking for something more than money.

> Make yourself so valuable in your work that eventually you will become indispensable. Exercise your privilege to go the extra mile, and enjoy all the rewards you receive. You deserve them.
>
> —OG MANDINO

I love this quote because it hits two leadership principles at the same time: Work hard and enjoy the rewards. Mandino says that people who achieve *deserve* the reward. That is so true. Leaders need to understand that followers *deserve* reward and recognition. This is more than money. It is the acknowledgment of their peers and the respect of their leaders. Making sure that they get that will create a satisfied and loyal group of people who call you their leader.

> For them to perceive the advantage of defeating the enemy, [your troops] must also have their rewards.
>
> —SUN TZU

Sun Tzu, the Chinese author of the *Art of War*, reminds us that if we want to get the most out of people, we must make sure they have their own rewards. Does it need to be a week at a four-star resort? No, but it needs to be commensurate with the work performed. If we ask people to undertake a small task, it makes sense to give them a small reward. If the task is a big one, then we should make sure that they are rewarded in a grand way. This helps ensure that they know that we appreciate their work and contribution.

> If you believe in yourself and have dedication and pride—and never quit, you'll be a winner. The price of victory is high but so are the rewards.
>
> —PAUL BRYANT

The price of victory is high. So true. And the bigger the victory, the bigger the price. The higher we set our sights the greater the price we will have to pay in order to get there. When we ask our people to make an extraordinary effort or pay a high price to achieve a great victory, we must make sure that they receive a reward that matches the effort. I believe that we should push our people to dream big dreams and attempt things that others think impossible. Let someone else be average. But at the same time, we need to make sure that we have great rewards to match the great price our people are willing to pay for the victory.

Questions for Reflection

- How well do you follow the rule of *You get what you reward?* Explain why you think so.
- Have you taken the time to understand what drives the people you lead so you can offer rewards other than money?
- Do you offer people the opportunity for public recognition of the efforts? If not, when will you start and how?

LEADERSHIP RULE NUMBER FOUR

YOU GET WHAT YOU WORK FOR

It still takes work. Work to set the expectations and model them, work to discover the best rewards and apply them, and beyond that, diligent work toward whatever goals and immediate targets you've set. To make leadership work:

- Set the standard high.
- Work harder, longer.
- Work hard *and* work smart.
- Overdeliver.

FOLLOWING THE RULE

Set the standard high. Most people live their lives as average. They live in the mediocre and the status quo. A quick look at the bell curve shows where most people live. That is true with people who hold positions of leadership. There is a big difference between holding a title of leader and being a true leader. I have had the good fortune of working with some great leaders. Many of them are looked at as though they stumbled upon it or got lucky. I have found that that is simply not true. Instead, those who achieve such greatness are the hardest workers you will ever know. They set the standard of work high for themselves and others. It isn't something they will do in the future. It is something they do every day. The standard is high whether they are leading at work or at home.

Work harder, longer. I have found that a lot of people are willing to work hard for a short period of time. But fewer are willing to work hard for their dreams day in and day out for years or decades. How many people have given up on their dreams before the breakthrough that would have happened? Countless millions. One of my friends always tells people not to quit before payday. Too many people work hard for a while, then they get discouraged, and then they quit. The unfortunate thing is that if they had worked harder for a little longer, they would actually have succeeded. Instead, they quit and had to start over. All too many people run through this cycle over and over again through their careers and never get to the reward. Stay with it. Don't quit.

Work hard and *work smart*. I have heard people say, "Work smart, not hard." Well, I don't think the two are mutually exclusive. In fact, you should do both. Yes, working smart is better than working hard. But working hard *and* smart is better than just working smart. As I have worked with successful leaders, I have found them to be the hardest-working people out there. I have some very successful people I work with who lead amazingly successful organizations. And one thing that is common to all of them is that they get to work early and they stay late. They aren't just calling it in. They work hard! Rarely does anyone become an overnight sensation. The fact is that behind most successful people you see hard work and discipline. They work smart *and* hard!

Overdeliver. There is an old saying that advises, "Underpromise and overdeliver." I think we need to change that. First of all, as great leaders, we shouldn't underpromise. That's a cop-out. We should boldly promise exactly what we expect to do. If you underpromise, you look like you're afraid of committing to a grand plan. If you overpromise you look like a person who can't execute. So just promise what you are going to do. Then overdeliver. Once the promise is made to your followers, work beyond imagination to make sure that what you deliver is far beyond what anyone ever expected. In doing that you gain the reputation of being the go-to person and one who gives more than anyone asked for.

MY FAVORITE QUOTES ON HARD WORK

The rewards go to the risk-takers, those who are willing to put their egos on the line and reach out to other people and to a richer, fuller life for themselves.
—SUSAN ROANE

I like this quote on risk because risk is hard. Risk is usually hard to make a decision on, hard to commit to, and hard to deliver on. It may not be physically hard, but it can be emotionally and psychologically hard on a leader. Stepping out and leading a group to take a risk is hard to do, but mandatory for the leader who is going to accomplish much and lead people to greatness.

> We will receive not what we idly wish for but
> what we justly earn. Our rewards will always be
> in exact proportion to our service.
> —EARL NIGHTINGALE

Nightingale reminds us that you get what you earn. You don't get what you deserve. You get what you earn. And the way you earn your reward is through good old-fashioned hard work. The same is true for leaders. You get what you earn over time through hard work. You will get the respect you earn. You will get the loyalty you earn. You will get the reward you earn. Your choice on how hard you will work will determine how much you earn, whether in dollars or anything else.

> I believe life is constantly testing us for our
> level of commitment, and life's greatest rewards
> are reserved for those who demonstrate a

never-ending commitment to act until they
achieve. This level of resolve can move moun-
tains, but it must be constant and consistent.

—TONY ROBBINS

One thing I have learned repeatedly is that life
is constantly testing our level of commitment. Life
is always presenting challenges to us that we must
overcome. The average leader gets to a place that
feels comfortable and then sits down to rest for
the long run. But the great leader understands that
we are always going to face challenges that will
stand as obstacles to our growth and the growth
of our organizations. The great leader looks at the
obstacle and resolves to work even harder, to
give even more effort, all with the goal of taking
the organization to the next level.

Don't judge each day by the harvest you reap,
but by the seeds you plant.

—ROBERT LOUIS STEVENSON

Ask a farmer about hard work. When I was
growing up, I used to spend some of my summers
in Nebraska with some relatives of my father. I
remember particularly my uncle Darrel and what

a hard worker he was. Funny thing about farming, though: you work and work and work, for months, without seeing anything. Just planting and working the ground. Watering. All that work that has to be done with virtually nothing to show for it. All for the hope that when the time comes a crop will pop up. As leaders, we can't just judge our work by the immediate results. Sometimes we are just planting and watering, and in the right time we will reap a harvest. But we can't forgo the hard work. If we don't do the hard work, we don't reap the harvest.

> It takes struggle, a goal and enthusiasm to make
> a champion.
> —NORMAN VINCENT PEALE

Who wants a struggle? I don't think many actually look for a struggle, but great leaders know that on the other side of the struggle is the victory. The more experienced I get the more I realize the valuable place of struggle in life. We spend our younger years trying to avoid struggle. Don't get me wrong, I am not suggesting that we should go looking for the struggle, but I am not so sure we should spend so much time avoiding it. Often, success is found on the other side of the struggle. Struggle makes us stronger and wiser. It is hard work, for sure. But the leader who is committed to persevering through the hard work of the struggle is the leader who will come out on top.

Questions for Reflection
- Be honest: How hard a worker are you?
- Are you committed to working harder?
- What seeds are you planting today that will produce a harvest later on?
- Do you have what it takes to push through the struggle?

──┤ ACKNOWLEDGMENTS ├──

Special acknowledgments to my agent, Matt Yates, and all the great folks at Jossey-Bass for their work in making this story become a reality. Thanks!

Chris Widener is a successful businessman, speaker, and author. An expert in leadership and personal development, Chris has extensive leadership experience in both the nonprofit and for-profit world. Chris's speaking engagements take him all over the world teaching people about leadership and influence. Chris's Ezine is one of the world's most widely distributed Ezines on leadership in the world.

Chris built and sold the only company to distribute personal and professional development audios through Costco and Sam's Club. He was also the co-host, along with Zig Ziglar, of the television show *True Performance*. He is the author of the *New York Times* and *Wall Street Journal* best-selling book *The Angel Inside*, as well as *The Art of Influence*.

For more information, please visit
www.ChrisWidener.com